STEAMBOATS ON THE
MISSISSIPPI

STEAMBOATS ON

FOURTH PRINTING

LIBRARY OF CONGRESS CATALOGUE CARD NUMBER: 62-10384

THE MISSISSIPPI

BY THE EDITORS OF
AMERICAN HERITAGE
The Magazine of History

NARRATIVE BY
RALPH K. ANDRIST

IN CONSULTATION WITH
C. BRADFORD MITCHELL
American Merchant Marine Institute

PUBLISHED BY
AMERICAN HERITAGE PUBLISHING CO., INC.
NEW YORK

BOOK TRADE AND INSTITUTIONAL DISTRIBUTION BY
HARPER & ROW

Foreword

The Mississippi is big and so is everything connected with it. It drains one of the world's largest watersheds. It has one of the longest valleys in the world—from the Rockies to the Gulf of Mexico. It has borne since the early 1800's the world's largest inland fleet. It has bred great men, great steamboats, and great legends—the first two often magnified by the third.

The Mississippi is violent. Its flood rampages, which we are only now learning to control, have drowned families, smashed towns, ruined farms, and sent lost packets lurching through business streets and cornfields. It has built and removed islands, undermined communities, lengthened and shortened its own course, even moved pieces of one state into another.

To most people "Mississippi" suggests "steamboat." Not that America's middle western waters were the only ones navigated by steam, or the first, or even necessarily the most important. But humanity is peculiar, and there is no accounting for what it chooses to forget and to remember. It has chosen—with the aid of TV and movies—to remember that "Mississippi" and "steamboat" go together. Hence, the average man of 1962, though he has never seen a steamboat, visualizes it in the special, unforgettable shape it took on the western rivers.

This book and its wealth of contemporary paintings and prints and rarely-seen photographs describe the Mississippi steamboat and the world through which it moved—a world the boats were largely responsible for bringing into being. It cannot of course tell the whole story. That, like the Mississippi itself, is too big. Mr. Andrist focuses on the so-called heyday of western steamboating, the nineteenth century's first seventy-five years.

The Mississippi story however does not end in 1875. The years since have brought a new galaxy of packet services, the perfection of the stern-wheeler, and a growth of river towing undreamt of in Mark Twain's day. We have seen the forty-six year career of the world's largest towboat, the 315-foot stern-wheeler *Sprague*, still preserved at Vicksburg. We have also seen the rise, and final withdrawal in 1961, of the side-wheel "transfer boats," which ferried whole trains across the Mississippi; and the evolution of the diesel towboat to the 9,000-horsepower quadruple-screw *America*, able to push forty-barge tows, rivaling in length and capacity the largest ocean-going cargo ships.

Today we are in the twilight of the steamboat age, 150 years after Nicholas Roosevelt took the historic *New Orleans* downriver through the chaos of the New Madrid Earthquake. The last side-wheelers appeared in 1925, the last stern-wheeler in 1940, and the last commercial steamers—twenty-one twin-screw towboats to meet the war emergency—in 1944. But a few river steamboats are still to be seen, even traveled on. They include a handful of upper Ohio stern-wheel towboats, three summertime excursion boats—the *Admiral*, the *Avalon*, and the *President*—and the stern-wheel cruising steamboat *Delta Queen*. When these last four go, Americans other than professional rivermen will lose their last chance of really knowing at first hand the bigness, power, and beauty of the Mississippi and its sister rivers.

C. BRADFORD MITCHELL

The New Orleans levee in 1853, the height of the Mississippi steamboat's golden era.

COVER: *A steamboat passing through the bayous at night is lighted by flaming torches.*
MUSEUM OF THE CITY OF NEW YORK

FRONT ENDSHEET: *This print of the bustling water front at St. Louis dates from 1859.*
COLLECTION OF STRATFORD LEE MORTON

BACK ENDSHEET: *A tobacco company issued this colorful advertising poster about 1860.*
MISSOURI HISTORICAL SOCIETY

This 1848 sketch of a steamboat calling at a tiny upriver settlement is by Seth Eastman.

Contents

ILLUSTRATED WITH PAINTINGS, PRINTS, DRAWINGS, MAPS, AND PHOTOGRAPHS OF THE PERIOD

1. The Year of Strange Happenings

In the Mississippi Valley 1811 was a year of marvels. The spring floods had been exceptionally high and the river had overflowed many miles beyond its banks. Then had followed the most serious outbreaks of sickness the river settlers could remember. For some strange, unknown reason, squirrels had begun to migrate southward in swarms that stopped at no obstacle; uncountable thousands died crossing the Ohio River. Then, during the summer, a great comet appeared night after night; its tail stretched across the sky, and to the superstitious it was an omen of disasters to come.

When autumn came, it brought an event even more terrifying. A great earthquake shook the central Mississippi Valley again and again, opening wide cracks in the earth, and rolling the ground in swells like the ocean. Parts of the banks of the Mississippi River collapsed and sank; in other

Pittsburgh, Pennsylvania (above), the birthplace of the Mississippi steamboat, was still a village in 1790 when this sketch was made. In 1811 Nicholas Roosevelt's famous New Orleans, *the first steamboat in the West, was built and launched at Pittsburgh.*

places the muddy river bottom rose where there had been deep channel.

And in the midst of this shuddering of the earth, the settlers of the still-wild western country were astonished to see a strange kind of boat puffing smoke and making its way down the river through floating trees uprooted by the earthquake. It was the first steamboat ever to float on a western river, and although most settlers had heard of the steam-driven vessels that had been operating on the Hudson River for several years, there were some ignorant folk who ran and hid. The Chickasaw Indians called it "Penelore," meaning fire-canoe, and the sparks and smoke from its stack convinced them that it was the comet of the summer returning.

Of all the strange events along the Mississippi in 1811, the most important by far was the appearance of the steam-driven boat. Its trip opened the most exciting, the busiest, and the most romantic period the Mississippi Valley has ever seen. After that passage, the great river was never the same again.

The captain of the boat was Nicholas J. Roosevelt, great-granduncle of Theodore Roosevelt, a man who had had some experience in steamboat construction and held patents on their machinery. Several steamboats were being operated on the Hudson River at that time by Robert Livingston and Robert Fulton, and Roosevelt had talked to the two men about the possibility of building steamboats west of the Allegheny Mountains for use on the Mississippi River. Livingston and Fulton were very much interested. They already had a monopoly on steamboat operation in New York and were interested in having the same control over transportation on western rivers. Nicholas Roosevelt would be their western representative.

But conditions on the Ohio and Mississippi were very different from those on the deep, slow-moving Hudson, so Roosevelt set out to learn about western rivers. He had a flatboat built at Pittsburgh and fitted out more elaborately than usual, because this was also going to be his honeymoon. His new bride, Lydia, was the daughter of the noted architect Benjamin Latrobe. In the spring of 1809, with his young wife and crew, Nicholas Roosevelt set off down the Ohio.

In 1809, the Ohio and the Mississippi areas were still the West. Settlements were small, few, and widely scattered, but on the river there was a heavy volume of produce being taken from the upper Ohio and its tributaries down to New Orleans. As they drifted downriver, Roosevelt talked to flatboatmen and keelboatmen. None of them gave him encouragement; they said the swift currents and shifting bottoms of the western rivers would make it impossible ever to use steam-powered boats of the kind he described. Roosevelt was not discouraged. He drifted on, studying currents and channels, so confident of bringing steamboats to these waters that when he found seams of coal on the banks of the Ohio, he hired men to open

A Frenchman who steamed upriver in 1820 abo the Maid of Orleans *painted the water colors on opposite page. At top is an Indian camp near the ri below it is the* Maid of Orleans, *the earliest kn picture of a Mississippi steamboat. The plan of Ro velt's* New Orleans *(below) is a modern re-creat*

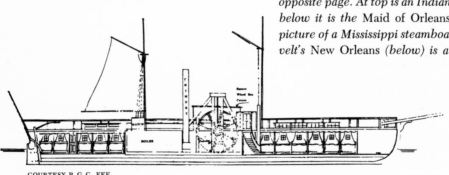

pendant mon voyage à St louis année 1820.

1 cabanne faite en écorce d'arbre &c

2 berceau d'enfant

3 orery dans un arbre pour piller la nuit &c

4 peaux de chevreuille appellée a sécher

No 1

Croquis d'un camp d'indien appellée Shawnay sur le Fleuve du missisippi

le 6 mars 1820

Steam boat Maid of Orleans on the Mississippy River Going to St Louis

Fleury Generelly 1.er
Eglee Generelly
Lovely Generelly
Edward Generelly

Parti le 1.er février 1820 de la N.lle Orléans
arrivé à St Louis le 4 août 1820 — 6 mois pour remonter

13

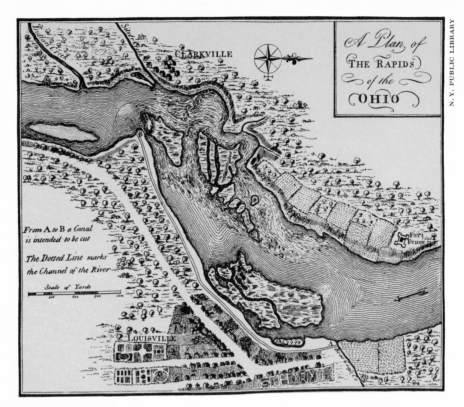

The map above shows the Rapids or Falls of the Ohio at Louisville, Kentucky, conquered in 1811 by the New Orleans. In the 1811 earthquake much of the water front of New Madrid, Missouri—shown below in 1826—crumbled into the river.

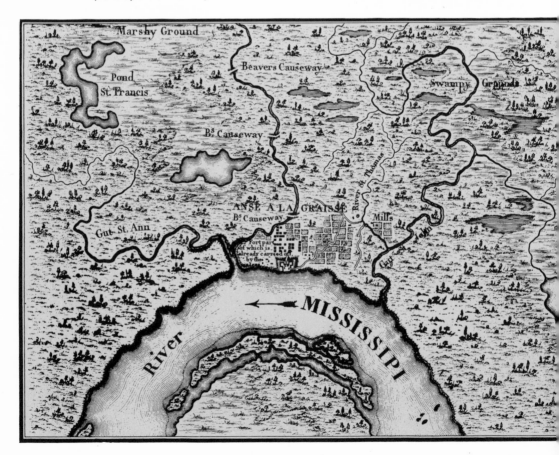

mines so there would be fuel for the steamboats when they did arrive.

He and Mrs. Roosevelt left their flatboat in New Orleans and returned to New York by ship. By spring, 1811, he was in Pittsburgh directing the building of a steamboat. There were difficulties: the boat yard was on low ground so that several times high water set his lumber afloat and once threatened to launch his boat when she was only half-finished. But in time she was completed, named the *New Orleans,* and properly launched.

We know little of what the *New Orleans* was like. She had a rounded hull and sat deep in the water. One account of the period describes her as about 148 feet long, which may be an exaggeration, and it is quite probable that—like Fulton's boats on the Hudson—she had two masts to carry sail in an emergency. It is also fairly certain that she was a side-wheeler because Roosevelt held patents on side paddle wheels.

When friends heard that Mrs. Roosevelt planned to go downriver on the new boat with her husband, they protested that it was impossible because she was soon to become a mother. But she had paid no attention when some of the same friends had told her, two years before, that it was not proper to go on a honeymoon trip to New Orleans on a flatboat, and she paid no attention now. When the *New Orleans* set out, in the fall, she was aboard.

The country through which they passed was still much as it had been before the first white man came, except for occasional settlers' clearings on the riverbanks. Between Pittsburgh and Natchez, Mississippi, there were only three towns of any size: Cincinnati, Ohio; Louisville, Kentucky; and New Madrid, Missouri. It is doubtful that any of them could have mustered two thousand souls in 1811. The people the Roosevelts had met when they came down the river on their flatboat were happy to see them again, and were much interested in their steamboat. But, they said, while this contraption puffing like a teakettle might be all very well coming downstream, it would never work upstream against the strong current.

Nicholas Roosevelt and his wife Lydia posed for this photograph with their grandson long after their voyage on the New Orleans.

When the boat stopped at Louisville, there was a delay. The town was situated at the head of the Falls of the Ohio—a long stretch of rapids where the river dashed over rock outcroppings and dropped twenty-two feet in two miles. Unless the river was high, limestone ledges threatened to rip the bottom out of any craft that attempted to run the Falls.

For the *New Orleans,* there was no question of trying to run the Falls. The water was not deep enough. While Roosevelt waited for the river to rise, he showed the citizens of Louisville what his steamboat could do, first in a short trip or two upstream, then in a run all the way against the current to Cincinnati. At the Falls, the river continued to swirl around the rock ledges; in the town of Louisville, Mrs. Roosevelt gave birth to her baby.

Then, at last, the river began to rise as a result of rains somewhere up on its tributaries, but the rise stopped after a few days. Veteran rivermen reported that there was just enough water to carry the *New Orleans* over the rock ledges, but shook their heads because it would require such skillful handling. After waiting a few days in vain to see whether the river would resume its rise, Roosevelt gave the order to take the steamboat down through the rapids. Mrs. Roosevelt re-

This detailed map of the lower Mississippi and some of its tributaries was drawn by a member of a British military expedition that went down the river in 1763. The officer who sketched it based it on earlier French maps.

fused to listen to those who wanted her and her new baby to go around the Falls by land; if her husband traveled on the *New Orleans,* so would she.

A pilot familiar with the Falls was taken aboard, the *New Orleans* headed into swift water, and everyone held his breath. The boilers were at full pressure; in order to navigate when running with the current, the boat had to move faster than the racing water. The ominous ledges of rock flashed by, sometimes fearfully close to the boat's hull, and disaster was avoided by mere inches a number of times until at last the *New Orleans* was safe below the rapids.

This frightening incident was scarcely past before another came. The boat was tied up below the Falls of the Ohio, with those aboard resting after their ordeal, when a sudden tremor shook the vessel, and some of those on her felt a sensation similar to seasickness. It was an experience that they would have many times in the weeks ahead, for this was the first shuddering of what would be called the New Madrid Earthquake, after the settlement that lay near its center.

As the *New Orleans* went on, down the lower Ohio and into the Mississippi, the earthquake grew worse. The land shook and rumbled, acres of riverbank sank into the river, islands disappeared, and new ones rose from the bottom. The pilot became completely confused in this changing, shifting river, and when he hailed flatboatmen to try to get his bearings, he found that they were as hopelessly lost as he was.

New Madrid, in that part of the country that would be Missouri in another ten years, was not only the largest settlement between Louisville and Natchez, but virtually the only one. It was a typical frontier collection of cabins and a few stores, with pigs and chickens wandering around the spaces between. Small as it had been, it had become even smaller by the time the *New Orleans* appeared in front of the town, for several cabins—some with their occupants—had been swallowed up by the collapsing riverbank. Even the graveyard was gone, caved into the river. Some of the residents had felled big trees at right angles to the direction in which the earth cracks were occurring and were clinging to them; if the ground opened under them they hoped the trees would bridge the chasms and keep them from falling in. Many people begged to be taken aboard the *New Orleans,* but there was no room, and Roosevelt had to pass them by and steam on down the debris-filled river.

Many stories have been told of the New Madrid Earthquake, the worst that ever struck the heart of North America in recorded times. Jets of gas and lumps of coals were thrown from under the bed of the river; great cracks appeared. A large section of land in the northwestern corner of Tennessee sank below the level of the Mississippi, and for hours the river below New Madrid ran backwards until the depression had been filled. That body of water is still there; it is known as Reelfoot Lake.

Roosevelt's pilot was completely lost, for the river had changed beyond all recognition. All he could do was to try to stay where the water was swiftest, because that usually indicated where the main channel and the deepest water were. However, care was needed where the channel swung near the bank, for there the current was eating away at the shore and there was danger of a cave-in while the *New Orleans* was passing, bringing down giant trees which could smash the boat.

One evening the boat was tied up to a tree at the foot of an island, and all night long those aboard were disturbed by the shock of floating objects hitting the hull. That puzzled them because the island should have protected them against objects drifting with the current. But when morning came they discovered the reason: there was no island. At first they thought the boat had come adrift, but a quick glance at the shore showed that they were not moving; the mooring line was still fast, but it led down into the water. The island had simply sunk into the river; the mooring line was cut with an axe to free the boat.

Fire caused another sort of scare one night. A servant, to dry some wood, had piled it too near the stove, and it caught fire. Luckily, someone awoke in time and gave the alarm, but much of the woodwork was destroyed before the flames were put out.

As the *New Orleans* moved south she left the earthquake region behind and at last reached Natchez. The engineer had let his fires get low just a little too soon in anticipation of stopping over, and as the vessel came in for a landing, the steam pressure dropped and the *New Orleans* began drifting helplessly downstream in sight of all the townspeople who had gathered on the river bluff to see their first steamboat. Quickly some kindling was fed into the furnace, the pressure climbed, and the pilot averted disaster and brought the boat in for a triumphant landing.

The final stage of the trip to New Orleans was made without further mishap, and was completed on January 10, 1812, some three and a half months after leaving Pittsburgh. Roosevelt immediately put the *New Orleans* into regular service carrying freight and passengers between New Orleans and Natchez, and then took a ship to the east coast to make further plans with Livingston and Fulton. He moved his family to Pittsburgh and was soon busy building more steamboats.

The *New Orleans,* first of a mighty line, hit a snag after two and a half years of service and sank. But by that time Fulton and Livingston had sent the *Vesuvius* and the *Aetna* from their Pittsburgh boat yard down to New Orleans; soon afterward the *Buffalo* joined them; and other men were building steamboats, too. The age of steam had reached the western waters.

Edouard de Montulé, a young Frenchman, visited the Mississippi in 1817 and kept illustrated notes on what he saw; his drawing above shows a small village near Natchez. The high bluffs above the village are a continuation of those on which Natchez was built. Montulé also included one of the river's famous snags (center) in his drawing. Joshua Shaw, an American artist, made the sketch below of women chatting with a backwoodsman on the banks of a western river about 1815.

This view of New Orleans was painted in 1803, the year the city and all of the Louisiana Territory became part of the United States. The prideful motto at top is held in the beak of an American eagle

This independent fur trader, sketched by nineteenth-century artist George Bingham, is headed up the Missouri River and into the Rockies to trap and to barter with the Indians for pelts.

2. Boats Before Steam

The big river was a main avenue of travel and trade long before the coming of the steamboat. The Indians had used it for uncounted centuries, and after the first white men had pushed into the West, trappers and fur traders moved about on the river and its branches, leading lives not much different from those of the red men. Then, after the Revolution, settlers had begun to cross the Allegheny Mountains, and for them the rivers provided a way to get their produce to market.

Once across the mountains, settlers found their natural allegiances turning from the East toward the West. They could no longer get their crops to eastern markets because only a few poor roads led back over the mountains. On the other hand, westward-flowing rivers at their doorstep provided smooth and ready highways. A farmer could build a flatboat from the trees on his land, load it with whatever he had to sell, and drift all the way down to New Orleans to sell his cargo at a good price. With any luck, he could probably sell the flatboat itself for a few dollars for the lumber in it.

Getting back home again, a thousand miles or more, had its problems and its dangers. Usually a flatboatman walked or went on horseback over the trail known as the Natchez Trace, which led from Natchez northeast into the Ohio Valley. But, except to men traveling together for protection, the Trace was extremely dangerous, a route frequented by the most murderous highwaymen and cutthroats who had not the slightest feeling about killing a traveler for his money. One way a man returning from New Orleans could avoid this peril (if he could afford the passage) was to take a keelboat upstream.

Keelboats, unlike flatboats, traveled upriver as well as down. They were well-designed and well-constructed craft, sixty to seventy feet long, fifteen to eighteen feet in beam, and three to four feet deep. The bow and stern were pointed, and the boats were roofed to protect cargo and passengers. Along each side, running the length of the boat, was a narrow gangway.

Going down the river, of course, was no problem in these long, slim boats, but returning against the current was the hardest kind of work and called for men with muscle and endurance. Where the water was not too deep, the boat was poled. Four or five men with long poles took places on the gangway near the bow but facing the stern. At a command, each man thrust one end of his pole against the river bottom, and leaning against the other end with his shoulder, walked toward the stern, thus pushing the keelboat ahead. When the line of men reached the stern, they walked rapidly forward again and repeated the process.

Where the water was too deep or the current too swift for poling, a tow-rope, called a cordelle, was used. This was tied to the top of the keelboat's thirty-foot mast to help it clear the brush along the bank; the cordelle itself was as much as a thousand feet long to reduce the tendency of the boat to be pulled in toward the shore. Along a river with ever-changing banks like the Mississippi, it was seldom possible to have anything resembling a tow-path, and it was sometimes necessary for men to go ahead and chop out brush that was in the way. If it was impossible to tow the boat, two or three men would carry the end of the rope up the river and tie it to a tree; the rest of the crew would then haul in the line and pull the keelboat forward, a process called warping.

Where the current was slight, the boatmen simply got out oars and rowed. Usually the keelboats carried a crude square sail, but in the twisting Mississippi, winds seldom came from the right direction for very long. Even

so, it must have been very pleasant to relax even for a few minutes after grueling hours of poling or towing.

Whereas a keelboat was built for easy handling, with rounded bottom and tapered ends, a flatboat was an awkward, square-ended, flat-bottomed, graceless scow, which could drift very well down a river but could hardly be moved a stone's throw upstream even with the most strenuous effort. Flatboats varied greatly in size. An average one was about fifty feet long and twelve to twenty feet wide.

A flatboat was roofed over in most cases, except for a few feet at each end, and the cargo was stored under this shelter. A great long oar, as much as fifty feet in length, projected from the stern for steering; there were one or two other oars on each side for rowing, and one in the bow for maneuvering in swift water and when making a landing. Ordinarily, a flatboat just drifted, and the side sweeps were used only to guide it away from an island or bar or in making a crossing where the channel swung from one side of the river to the other. (Because these side sweeps projected outward like horns, flatboats were often called "broadhorns.")

The river produced its own kind of people, but its most distinctive breed were the keelboatmen. Because they got into more fights and drank more and put up with more hardships than any other men on the river, the keelboatmen looked upon themselves as a race apart—superior to all others. They

The fun-loving Missouri flatboatmen above, painted about 1857 by George Bingham, are having a celebration at the end of a journey downriver. The keelboat in the 1832 print below is taking advantage of a prevailing wind to head up the Mississippi under sail rather than being poled.

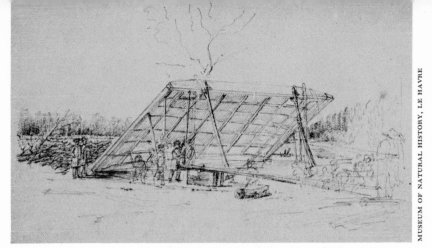

Flatboats and keelboats once virtually covered the Mississippi and its tributaries. The sketch above shows the way a flatboat was built; at right, a settler's flatboat, jammed with livestock, heads down the Ohio; and in the side view of a keelboat below, the passengers take the air. The crew of the keelboat at the bottom is hauling their craft upriver with a long rope or cordelle.

were strong, hard as nails, loud, fear-less, and tremendous and tiresome braggarts. They called themselves "half-horse—half-alligator"; they loved to fight, and when there was no one else to fight with, they would battle each other just for the fun of it. These combats were brutal affairs in which fists, feet, knees, and teeth were used; and if a thumb gouged out an oppo-nent's eye, that was part of the game. When keelboats landed in a river town, peaceable citizens tried to keep out of the way.

The keelboatmen's particular hero was named Mike Fink. Mike, accord-ing to the stories, could outfight, out-shoot, outdrink, and outwork any man on the river. All boatmen of his time made the most outrageous statements about their capabilities; each one had his own brag telling how rough, tough, and mean he was. This he recited, often as a challenge, while strutting, puffing out his chest, whooping, jump-ing into the air and knocking his heels together, and otherwise carrying on in a way that looked silly to more civi-lized people—although they were care-ful not to say so out loud.

Many versions of Mike Fink's brag have come down to us, but all of them make the same sort of claims: "Hurray for me, you scapegoats! I'm a land-screamer—I'm a water-dog—I'm a snapping turtle—I can lick five times my own weight in wildcats. I can use up Injuns by the cord. I can out-run, out-dance, out-jump, out-dive, out-drink, out-holler, and out-lick any

white thing in the shape o' human that's ever put foot within two thou-sand miles o' the big Massassip. I'm a Salt River roarer, I love the wimmin, and I'm chock full o' fight. . . ."

Some of the Mike Fink story is pure invention, and some is probably the adventures of other rivermen which were attributed to Mike, and part is undoubtedly true, but it is difficult to tell where the truth begins and ends. Mike Fink followed the river from about 1790 to 1822. Before that, be-ginning when he was seventeen, he was a scout—one of a group of rangers that kept watch on the Indians at a time when the frontier was only fifty miles or so west of Pittsburgh. The scouts went out alone, traveling silent-ly through the woods deep in Indian country. Many stories were told about Mike's daring and resourcefulness. Once, for instance, he was stalking a deer when he caught sight of an In-dian intent on the same prey. He si-lently stalked the Indian while the latter stalked the animal, and when the Indian took aim, so did Mike. As the Indian fired at the deer, Mike fired at the same instant—at the Indian. Then he collected both the Indian's scalp and the choice parts of the deer.

But Mike Fink soon gave up scout-ing and turned to keelboating, which proved to be his real element. He was known as the Snapping Turtle on the Ohio and the Snag on the Mississippi, and on both he was the foremost of the men who were half-horse—half-alligator. Although Mike was a good

This handsome painting, done about 1800, shows a Mississippi River plantation in Louisiana called White Hall. A flatboat (left rear) has tied up at the plantation landing; another one is at the right. The two sailing vessels at center are keelboats—the one in the middle of the river is carrying bales of cotton, while the one with the elegant canopy is a pleasure craft.

boatman, there was one kind of commodity that could not be safely left in his keeping. Once when he was long overdue in Pittsburgh, a man was sent down the Ohio to find him. When finally located, Mike was very vague about the cause of the delay and promised, without much enthusiasm, that he would try to get started the next morning. The man from Pittsburgh slept aboard the keelboat that night (Mike had not seemed very enthusiastic about that, either) and was wakened later by mysterious whisperings and movings about. He crept to where he could see what was going on—and discovered why Mike and his crew had made such a leisurely trip. Part of the cargo was brandy; each night the boatmen had been drilling a hole in a cask, removing part of the liquor, and refilling the cask with water.

The steamboat soon put most of the keelboats out of business; human muscle could not compete with steam in moving a boat upstream. For a long while, however, keelboatmen continued to work the thinly settled upper part of the changeable Missouri and several other tributaries, particularly during periods of low water. But on the lower Mississippi it did not take long; within eleven years after Nicholas Roosevelt brought the *New Orleans* down the river, even the king of the keelboatmen had given up.

Mike Fink had gone up the Missouri —as a trapper, not a boatman—where he was drinking far more whiskey than even his powerful body could stand.

29

Living up to his brag of being half-horse—half-alligator, this wild-eyed boatman from the pages of the humorous Davy Crockett's Almanack *of 1840 is driving a team of sea serpents down a turbulent western river.*

He died, as did so many men in the West, from a bullet. Details of the story differ, but apparently Mike was playing the favorite keelboatmen's game of "shooting the cup," in which two men took turns shooting a tin cup filled with whiskey off each other's heads. Mike, who had never missed anything in his life, who could drive a nail with a rifle ball, this time shot two inches too low. He was very drunk, it is true, but never in the past had any amount of liquor seemed to affect his almost unbelievable marksmanship. Many of the other men at the fur post believed he had killed on purpose and later, in an argument, one of them shot Fink.

It is harder to fit flatboatmen into a pattern. They were a mixed lot. Some of them were farmers, taking the produce of their own and sometimes a neighbor's farm down to New Orleans; perhaps they never made more than one or two trips. Abraham Lincoln, as a young man, hired himself out for two such trips. Some boats carried families of settlers on their way to make new homes in the West. And there were also professional flatboatmen, for often owners of a valuable cargo liked to hire a man who knew the river and how to handle a flatboat.

The keelboatmen looked down on the men in the flatboats, but the latter could be tough, too. In 1842 a crew member of a flatboat tied up at Memphis was killed while resisting arrest, and the crews of five hundred other boats moored there marched on the town and tried to burn and loot it. They were always troublesome in New Orleans when their long journey ended and they had money in their pockets and nothing to do but enjoy themselves. They liked to wreck respectable restaurants and theaters, and bands of them often engaged in wild battles.

The steamboat did not bring an end to flatboating as it had to keelboating. In fact, the number of flatboats increased until as late as 1847, when over 2,700 came down the Mississippi. A farmer with a harvest of pumpkins and Indian corn and a load of barrel staves often could not afford to send his cargo to market by steamboat, so he bought or made a flatboat, often in partnership with some of his neighbors, and let the current take his produce downriver to New Orleans.

A New Englander named Timothy Flint, who traveled the Mississippi in 1826, described the varied cargoes of the flatboats. In the spring they came down the river in fleets; one hundred of them were counted tying up in one day just below New Madrid, a favored stopping place. They came from dozens of tributary streams, bringing planks from the pine forests of southwestern New York, pork, flour, whiskey, hemp, tobacco, and rope from Kentucky and Tennessee, plus cotton, also from Tennessee. Missouri and Illinois sent horses and cattle; from Missouri, too, came lead and furs. Some boats carried corn, others barrels of potatoes and apples and cider; there were dried fruits, many kinds of liquor, and a whole catalogue of other items. There were boats with chickens on the roofs; there were boats from which came the squealing of pigs, the lowing of cattle, the stamping of horses. There were boats fitted out for nothing but the carrying of turkeys and loaded down with the gobbling birds.

Flint also told of a boat which carried a large tinsmith's shop. It stopped at a river settlement until it had sold all the pots and pans it could, then it was floated down to the next town. Another had a shop aboard for manufacturing axes, scythes, and other iron tools, as well as for the shoeing of horses; still others were fitted out as dry goods stores.

Then there were flatboats of emigrants on their way to settle in the lower Ohio Valley. One writer tells of

Mike Fink, king of the keelboatmen.

seeing two large boats drift by, each eighty or ninety feet long, lashed together, and carrying several New England families. They were open scows except for a small house on each, and on each was a haystack at which several horses and cattle were feeding. Plows, wagons, pigs, chickens, and children were scattered around as they would be in a farmyard. One woman was washing clothes at a washtub; an old lady with spectacles on her nose sat knitting on a chair at the door of one of the cabins, and the men sat around chewing tobacco and talking. It looked more like a quiet farm scene than the deck of a boat out on the Mississippi.

The river also saw the shanty boats which appeared in large numbers when the riverbanks became settled.

A poor relative of the flatboat, it was used by people more interested in living an easy life on the river than in getting places or hauling things. A shanty boat was usually made of boards and timbers fished from the river, and was a square scow about twenty by ten or twelve feet with a small house covering most of the deck space. Floating downriver through the spring and summer was pleasant, and when fall came the shanty-boatman was in a warmer climate. He tied his boat up in some quiet creek and spent the winter trapping and fishing and stealing a pig or two if the chance presented itself. When spring came, he floated on down to New Orleans, sold his furs, and then returned up the Mississippi and Ohio, there to build another shanty boat and start the pleasant trip all over again.

Among the shanty-boat people were menders of pots and pans, grocers and saloonkeepers, cobblers, barbers, and others who brought goods and services that were welcomed in the small, isolated settlements where the outside world seldom reached. There were also small showboats (the large ones were towed by steamboat), and one man wrote of seeing a circus boat with a twenty-five-foot ring on deck, with performing horses, acrobats, and trapeze artists. These floating shows appeared as settlements grew along the rivers, and they were still active years after the Civil War.

And, it should be added, many of the shanty-boat types were rascals who could turn with complete ease to chicken stealing, to selling patent medicine, to being fourth-rate actors, or even pretending to be preachers if

33

it appeared that a fire-and-brimstone sermon might bring in a nice collection. Mark Twain, in *Huckleberry Finn*, wrote of two such rapscallions, the Duke of Bilgewater and the Late Dauphin, who were willing to do any outrageous thing if it meant personal gain. These two were not entirely creatures of Twain's imagination; he knew the river and its people, and the Duke and Dauphin were modeled after rascals he had heard of or known.

The steamboatmen had to share the river with the people who drifted on it without steam, but they never came to like each other. Mark Twain writes

Once steamboats came to the rivers, flatboats like this one ran the great danger of being run down in the dark or in heavy river fog.

of their feud in *Life on the Mississippi:* "Of course, on the great rise, down came a swarm of prodigious timber-rafts from the head waters of the Mississippi, coal barges from Pittsburgh, little trading scows from everywhere, and broad-horns from 'Posey County,' Indiana, freighted with 'fruit and furniture'—the usual term for describing it, though in plain English the freight thus aggrandized was hoop-poles and pumpkins. Pilots bore a mortal hatred to these craft; and it was returned with usury. The law required all such helpless traders to keep a light burning, but it was a law that was often broken. All of a sudden, on a murky night, a light would hop up, right under our bows, almost, and an agonized voice, with the backwoods 'whang' to it, would wail out:

" 'Whar'n the ——— you goin' to! Cain't you see nothin', you dash-dashed aig-suckin', sheep-stealin', one-eyed son of a stuffed monkey!'

"Then for an instant, as he whistled by, the red glare from our furnaces would reveal the scow and the form of the gesticulating orator as if under a lightning-flash, and in that instant our firemen and deck-hands would send and receive a tempest of missiles and profanity, one of our wheels would walk off with the crashing fragments of a steering-oar, and down the dead blackness would shut again. . . ."

However, it should be remembered that Mark Twain was a steamboat pilot and could hardly be expected to say a good word for a flatboatman.

In 1825 the keelboat Philanthropist *started down the Ohio, loaded with settlers bound for New Harmony, Indiana; aboard was Charles Lesueur, a French naturalist, who made these fine drawings of keelboat life. Above, the boat is delayed by a floating bridge in the frozen river; at right, under way again. The sketches below show the settlers' cramped life, especially at mealtime (below right).*

3. The Great River

This modern photograph of the Mississippi was taken near St. Louis, Missouri. The structures built out into the broad, winding stream are wing dams designed to keep the unruly current of the river from shifting or filling in the channel used for shipping.

Just about everything concerning the Mississippi and its family of tributary streams is on a grand scale. Its drainage basin reaches from within 225 miles of the Atlantic to within 500 miles of the Pacific and includes all or parts of thirty-two states and, for good measure, parts of two Canadian provinces. It is not the largest drainage basin in the world—that of the Amazon is much greater, and the Congo basin has a slight edge—but beyond all arguing, its combination of soil, climate, and other resources is more hospitable to mankind than any other of the world's great river valleys.

The Mississippi-Missouri, considered as one river, is the former champion of the world as far as length is concerned. It is difficult to put a yardstick to a crooked, constantly changing river, but a recent and dependable measurement indicates that the Nile is 4,053 miles long and the Mississippi-Missouri 3,986. The Army engineers, in their work of improving navigation on the river, have shortened the Mississippi by a great many miles; otherwise, the longest river would still be in America instead of in Africa.

There are good reasons why many geographers consider the Mississippi-Missouri to be one river. The Missouri is longer, has a greater drainage basin, and in most seasons carries more water than the upper Mississippi. An explorer coming up the Mississippi and reaching the Missouri when it is in either its normal or flood stage (when it is dry, the Missouri can be a puny

37

trickle) would be certain that this was the main stream.

Why, then, did explorers choose the lesser branch? Because they did not come up the river. They were Frenchmen who came from the Great Lakes overland and started their exploration of the Mississippi from the north. When they saw other rivers join the Mississippi farther south, even the great Missouri and Ohio, they treated them as mere branches.

The French explorers from the north also brought a name with them. The river had been called many things from time to time by the Spanish, the English, and the many Indian tribes living along it. But the tribes the French met in the north all referred to it as the Great River, even though they knew it when it was a baby compared to what it would become. These tribes all belonged to the great Algonkian family, and their languages, while different, were related; some said "Mitchisipi," others "Missi-sipi," still others "Mis-ipi," but all meant Great River. The French made it Mississippi, and so it remained.

It is not true, as so many believe, that Mississippi means Father of Waters. The French first made that mistake in translating from the Indian name. But Father of Waters is also a good name, one that describes the mighty river with a touch of poetry.

The Mississippi is born where it flows out of Lake Itasca in Minnesota, a clear sparkling brook, a bit too broad for leaping but easy to wade. During

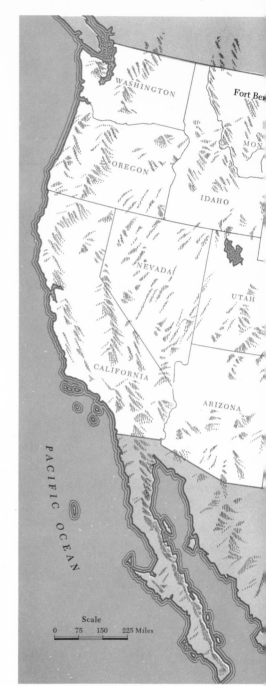

DAVID GREENSPAN

THE MISSISSIPPI
AND ITS TRIBUTARIES

The mighty Mississippi-Missouri river system, lying between the Appalachian mountain chain in the east and the Rockies in the west, drains 1,240,000 square miles—an area nearly one-third the size of the entire nation, including Alaska and Hawaii, and more than five times the size of France. The combined Mississippi-Missouri is 3,986 miles long, equal to the distance between New York and Berlin. The map includes the major tributary streams as well as the more important river towns and geographical features associated with the Great River.

39

The Olivier plantation, painted in 1861, was a sugar plantation in the Louisiana bayou country. The sugar cane was processed in the red refinery building at right. The fashionable dresses and the peacocks typify the elegance of pre-Civil War plantation life.

its early journey it runs over clear gravel bottoms and through several large lakes before it leaves the pine country and plunges over the Falls of St. Anthony at Minneapolis.

Below the Falls, the river begins to gather strength as the tributaries flow in, the Minnesota River and the St. Croix, the Black and the Wisconsin, the Iowa and the Rock, the Des Moines and the Illinois, and many more. Here it flows between high, rocky bluffs seldom more than a mile apart, offering some of the nation's most beautiful scenery. Its water is relatively clear, but just above St. Louis the Missouri River—the "Big Muddy"—pours in, and the river is clear no more.

Less than two hundred miles farther downstream, the Ohio enters from the east. Its waters seem reluctant to mix with those of the Mississippi, and the blue-green Ohio water stays on the east side of the river, and the brown Mississippi water on the other, with a definite line dividing them. At times, the difference can be seen for many miles downriver.

The mouth of the Ohio is usually taken as the point that marks the division between the upper and the lower Mississippi. There are no more of the beautiful rocky bluffs here; the banks are now low and sometimes swampy, and they become more so farther down the river. Only in a very few places does the river run into high land as it meanders back and forth in its great plain. These bluffs were ideal for forts when nations were struggling for control of this great country; later they were equally prized as the locations for towns because they were above flood waters. Memphis, Tennessee, and Vicksburg and Natchez in Mississippi occupy the three such spots on the east bank; New Madrid, Missouri, and Helena, Arkansas, are the two on the west bank.

The lower river usually ranges between about half a mile to almost a mile wide, occasionally broadening to a mile and a half or more, and it averages from fifty to a hundred feet deep. It is an awe-inspiring sight, this expanse of moving water, full of strange eddies and sudden boilings, coming from around the bend upstream and disappearing around the bend below, mighty and unceasing and unstoppable, and yet working silently except for the suck and gurgle where it eats away at a bank or swirls around a half-submerged dead tree.

An oddity about this lower river: in most places, it is about as high as the land on both sides. Over the centuries the river bed and the land immediately on both sides of it have been building up with the silt brought from upriver. As a result, the river has become too high for a great deal of

This decorative map includes all of the plantations located on the Mississippi between New Orleans and Natchez in 1858. The map is split in half: the left half covers the area from Natchez (top) to West Baton Rouge; the right half continues southward from West Baton Rouge to New Orleans at the bottom.

PLANTATIONS
ON THE
MISSISSIPPI RIVER
FROM NATCHEZ TO NEW ORLEANS
1858

Lake Itasca, Minnesota (above), is pictured in 1832 when it was discovered as the source of the Mississippi by a party of explorers led by Henry Schoolcraft; the unexpected visitors are being greeted by local Indians. Balize, painted below in the 1820's, was a small community built on pilings at the mouth of the Mississippi that was used until the 1860's as a place for taking on and dropping off the expert river pilots who guided boats up and down the Great River. It was named for the balise or beacon light established there by the French in 1700.

neighboring land to drain into it very well; there are great stretches along the river, scores of miles wide, laced with swamps, sluggish rivers, streams without purpose, and connecting bayous, a land whose waters have no place to flow. It hardly need be said that a river like this is not a good neighbor in floodtime.

The river is always changing, gnawing away one bank, building another, building itself islands and bars, or taking them away. Mark Twain writes in *Life on the Mississippi* of how he came back to visit the river twenty-one years after he had left it. As a pilot, he had known every bar and island in the river, but now, as his boat neared Cairo, Illinois, going downriver, everything was changed:

"I could recognize big changes from Commerce [Missouri] down. Beaver Dam Rock was out in the middle of the river now, and throwing a prodigious 'break;' it used to be close to the shore, and boats went down outside of it. A big island that used to be away out in mid-river, has retired to the Missouri shore, and boats do not go near it any more. The island called Jacket Pattern is whittled down to a wedge now, and is booked for early destruction. Goose Island is all gone but a little dab the size of a steamboat. The perilous 'Graveyard,' among whose numberless wrecks we used to pick our way so slowly and gingerly, is far away from the channel now, and a terror to nobody. . . .

"Near the mouth of the river several islands were missing—washed away. Cairo was still there—easily visible across the long, flat point upon whose further verge it stands; but we had to steam a long way around to get to it. Night fell as we were going out of the 'Upper River' and meeting the floods of the Ohio. We dashed along without anxiety; for the hidden rock which used to lie right in the way has moved up stream a long distance out of the channel; or rather, about one county has gone into the river from the Missouri point, and the Cairo point has 'made down' and added to its long tongue of territory correspondingly. The Mississippi is a just and equitable river; it never tumbles one man's farm overboard without building a new farm just like it for that man's neighbor. This keeps down hard feelings."

This habit of the river of shifting its course, of eroding one shore and building up another and so sliding sideways, cost a good many farmers their fields, as Twain pointed out. Sometimes it was hard on entire towns. Some of these were small and did not matter much—except to the people who lived in them. Others were not so small—such as Napoleon, Arkansas.

Napoleon was located where the Arkansas River joins the Mississippi. The two rivers took their time chewing away the town. Each time the owner of a building on the river side of town grew nervous about the river becoming too close a neighbor, he would build again on the far side of town and let the river take the old

place. But the river just kept coming, and after six years, the citizens decided enough was enough, and moved out to the last man. Napoleon had been the county seat with, among other things, a big government hospital, but all of it went to the catfish.

New Madrid, Missouri, the town so badly shaken by the earthquake of 1811, still exists as a small town on its bluff above the river, but only because its citizens kept moving it back. The river never stopped eating away at the bank in front of the town, and again and again the threatened buildings were hauled back to safer ground. At one time, buildings were kept on rollers for easier moving. The site of the New Madrid of 1811, where the frightened people stood to watch the *New Orleans,* is now under water, over near the Kentucky shore.

The Mississippi is a remarkably

During floodtime the angry waters of the Mississippi often broke through the levees, forming deep cuts called crevasses. The men in this 1891 photograph are trying to repair, with earth and sandbags, a levee that has been badly damaged by a wide crevasse.

crooked river, throwing itself into deep bends and curves which, with time, are cut deeper and deeper. Horseshoe curves are formed that may eventually become fifteen or twenty miles around, but only a mile or so across the narrow neck. Sometimes, on a night when the river is high, the water breaks through the neck in a stream that is small at first but grows larger by the minute as the current claws at the sides of the cut. The earth drops in, as much as an acre at a time, with any houses, barns, fences, cattle, or humans unlucky enough to be in the way. Full-grown trees tumble along like straws. Then, within a day or so, the new channel has widened enough so that the current loses some of its force, and the river settles down to business in a new location.

As for the old channel, it is now an "oxbow lake," and any plantation which was on it is now far from the river—and in the steamboat days, worth a great deal less than before the cutoff.

The river is at its most fearful in floodtime. The water may rise as much as fifty feet and more; the current becomes a wild, irresistible tide. Huge trees go racing by, tossed end-over-end. Planks, rowboats, dead animals, sheds and cabins, a thousand kinds of debris are carried along. The river spreads far over its banks, sometimes until it becomes fifty miles or more wide. Today, elaborate levees and other flood control works usually hold the river in check, but a hundred years ago the protecting levees were few and small, and the Mississippi usually went where it wanted to go.

Rivermen had a special kind of hate for the trees that settled themselves into the river bottom when banks crumbled into the water. Sometimes, of course, they rotted away harmlessly, but all too often they became the worst kind of menaces to boats. When a forest giant slid into the stream, the great weight of earth still clinging to its roots sank to the bottom. Mud and silt collected around the roots, and soon the tree became firmly set on the bottom, more or less upright. The buffeting of floating logs and other debris would break off smaller branches, making it harder for a steamboat pilot to see, and the tree became another dangerous snag, ready to rip open the bottom of an unfortunate boat.

Sometimes, though, the tree did not become rigidly embedded in the bottom but became fastened in such a way that the elasticity of its roots let it bob with the current. The tree was pushed under by the powerful flow of water; then its buoyancy brought it to the surface again, where it was shoved under once more. Such objects were called "sawyers," and boatmen hated them even more than they did snags. Their bobbing up and down had a definite rhythm that sometimes took a number of minutes; a steamboat pilot coming around a bend would see nothing but clear water ahead of him, and then, when it was too late to stop, the great, dripping branches of a sawyer would break through the water and rise up like a bony hand in front of the boat—and another side-wheeler would be lost to the river.

Most of the Mississippi's numerous family of tributaries were much like their parent. Here and there one runs through rock or gravel, but usually their banks are dirt and clay which makes for crooked, changing channels.

A sawyer, one of the worst menaces in the river.

Steamboats ran aground on bars and crashed into snags in the Wabash and Cumberland and Minnesota rivers just as they did on the Mississippi, though in fewer numbers.

But the Missouri deserves special mention because it makes the Mississippi look like the tamest kind of a stream. It is certainly one of the world's most changeable rivers. From the heavy load of mud it carries it is always building up new sand bars and islands and then taking them away. The banks are constantly being eaten away or built up; they seldom stay as they are. And it is a great river for cut-offs; it is forever swinging wide loops and then deciding some night when the water is high that it wants to go across the neck. They say that if a Missouri River farmer in town is asked how things are, he will immediately look uneasy and head for home to make sure the river has not taken his farm while he was gone. One other thing about the Missouri: it is not called the Big Muddy for nothing. On an average day, it carries 275,000 tons of soil past Omaha, Nebraska. But in floodtime, it is really loaded with silt: then one cubic foot of its water contains forty-two pounds of dirt!

This silt, and that carried in by hundreds of other streams, east and west, finally comes to rest where the Mississippi meets the Gulf of Mexico. Here the Mississippi is a weary stream. Its current slows down; it can no longer carry its load of mud, which drops to the bottom. In a century and

The huge river system formed by the Missouri and Mississippi flows through sharply contrasting terrain. The rugged upper Missouri area (above) was a land of buffalo herds and roaming Indians when western artist George Catlin painted it in the 1830's. The 1840 painting at right by an unknown American artist shows the low Mississippi bayou country.

a half, the river has added about fifty square miles of land to Louisiana. About one hundred miles below New Orleans the Great River ends in a flat land of mud that barely rises above the sea. Here is where the water from Lake Itasca in Minnesota, and from a point more than eight thousand feet high on the border of Montana, and from West Virginia and New York and a multitude of other places finally joins the salt water.

4. Engine on a Raft

Henry Shreve was a get-things-done kind of man. When he became interested in steamboating, he just went ahead and built a steamboat. He had grown up on rivers, traveling by canoe and keelboat in the western country when he was still in his teens. In 1808 he had opened the fur trade between Philadelphia and St. Louis, and he had broken the British monopoly over the trade in lead from mines in the Mississippi Valley.

Now, late in 1814, he was bringing a steamboat named the *Enterprise* down to New Orleans. One problem confronted him: the Fulton and Livingston interests, that had brought the first steamboats to the Mississippi,

claimed a monopoly on all such craft operating on the lower river, and Shreve had not gotten a license from them or paid them anything.

Captain Henry Shreve and his *Enterprise* reached New Orleans in the midst of a great deal of excitement. The War of 1812 was still being fought, and an attack by the British was feared. Shreve and his boat immediately went to work hauling supplies for General Andrew Jackson's army. When the British did come, he tied up the *Enterprise* long enough to take command of a 24-pounder cannon during the Battle of New Orleans. After he went back to steamboating, the Fulton-Livingston group tried to have his boat seized by

Captain Henry M. Shreve (above) pioneered Mississippi River steamboating. The old woodcut on the opposite page shows a boiler explosion aboard Shreve's steamboat Washington *in 1816.*

court order for violation of their monopoly, but Shreve was able to retain possession while the case was being decided and went on operating her.

That spring, 1815, he set out on a trip upriver. The Fulton-Livingston people had three boats in service, but so far none of them had gone farther upriver than Natchez. Now Captain Shreve took the *Enterprise* all the way up to Louisville in what was considered the almost incredibly short time of twenty-five days. Then, for good measure, he kept on, past Pittsburgh and on to Brownsville on the Monongahela, reaching there in July after a fifty-four-day trip from New Orleans.

While the 2,200-mile trip was a notable one for an early steamboat, a riverman like Henry Shreve saw that neither the Fulton boats nor his *Enterprise* were right for western rivers. Their hulls were deep and rounded, as proper boat hulls always had been, but the western streams often became dangerously shallow—in many places several inches of water could mean the difference between a steamboat's crossing a bar or getting hung up for hours. The Fulton boats worked well

on deep, slow eastern rivers like the Hudson; the Mississippi was another kind of stream altogether.

What was needed was a boat that would draw less water, one that would move *on* the water instead of through it. The solution was a wide, shallow hull, with the heavy boilers and machinery atop the hull instead of within it. Such a boat was not invented in one burst of inspiration; instead, this idea (which skeptics snorted at as an engine on a raft) evolved slowly. Captain Shreve took an important first step toward such a steamboat with his *Washington*, built in 1816.

The *Washington*'s hull was not radically different from other boats of the time, but Shreve made two important changes: he decked over the hull and placed the heavy boilers on this deck; and he replaced the bulky low-pressure engine used by the Fulton boats with a high-pressure engine of a new design. Not only did it produce the greater power needed against the strong currents of western streams, but it was much lighter. Shreve did away with the heavy condenser that allowed the same water to be used over

Snags like this one were grim warnings to pilots.

and over. Why save on water, he asked, when the boat was running on a whole river of it? Above the boilers was a second deck, where the accommodations for passengers were.

The *Washington*'s immediate success set other designers to work. Hulls became shallower, and soon high-pressure engines were placed on the first deck along with the boilers. If any one craft can be called the "father of western steamboats," it is probably Captain Henry Shreve's *Washington*.

The *Washington* reached New Orleans in the fall and showed in every way that she was indeed superior to the Fulton boats. Once again, the Fulton-Livingston group was waiting with its claims of monopoly and tried to have the *Washington* seized, but Shreve was able to retain possession of her, as he had the *Enterprise*, until

the case could be decided in court, and the next spring, 1817, he took the *Washington* up to Louisville. The boat performed perfectly, making the trip in twenty-five days, which was looked on then as a scorching speed.

The *Washington*'s record has its dark side, too, for it provided America with its first steamboat disaster. On her maiden voyage a boiler had exploded, blowing Shreve and most of his crew overboard and killing thirteen. Such a fate would overtake a great many steamboats in the years ahead.

Captain Shreve continued his fight against the monopoly. It took all his

This photograph of the Red River "raft" was taken in 1873. Despite Captain Henry Shreve's destruction of the tangled raft with his snag boats in the 1830's, it re-formed and was not completely eliminated until 1880.

COLLECTION OF LEONARD V. HUBER

money during the three years it was carried through the courts, until finally the monopoly was broken. The way was open for any man with ambition and enterprise to become a steamboat owner on a western river.

Captain Henry Shreve did other things for steamboating. One was to concern himself with the problem of snags. As the number of boats increased, so did the number of accidents caused by running onto snags.

Shreve felt sure he could do something about this danger. It took several years before he could get the government to help because a good many people growled about wasting public money on foolish schemes, but finally he was able to go ahead. His snag boat, the *Heliopolis*, was an odd craft. She had two hulls, about ten feet apart, connected halfway back. In the front was a massive wedge-shaped beam, a sort of battering ram. The vessel was braced and cross-braced with stout timbers to make it as sturdy as possible, and it had other special equipment such as a hoist for dragging logs aboard, rollers on which to move them, and the like. Shreve brought her down into the Mississippi in the late summer of 1829, and he moved at once toward a place called Plum Point, the worst stretch on the entire river—a terror to boatmen, where the snags waited like teeth for any craft that wandered a little outside the crooked channel. He had an audience, too—the crews of flatboats, rafts, and steamboats who stood by to watch and laugh at what could not help but be a failure.

Captain Shreve selected a large snag and drove the boat straight at it. They came together with a crash, but it was the snag that gave way; the stoutly built *Heliopolis* was not harmed at all. The fallen snag was hoisted aboard the boat, cut into pieces too short to cause any more trouble, and allowed to float away. When a snag lay too far below the surface for the ram to catch it, a chain suspended between the two hulls was dropped to catch it as the boat surged forward. Again and again Shreve drove his boat ahead until Plum Point was free of snags and the men who had come to guffaw were convinced.

For more than a dozen years Captain Shreve pulled snags from the river under government contract. As part of his work, he attacked the famous Red River "raft." This was a tangle of dead trees and other floating debris which choked the Red River for perhaps 160 miles in Louisiana and Arkansas. In places this mass was jammed so tightly, with soil collected on it, that it supported all kinds of plants, even full-size trees; horsemen are said to have ridden across it without the slightest suspicion that a river surged beneath.

Captain Shreve went to work on it in 1833, using several government snag boats of the kind he had invented. Logs were pulled away from the downstream side of the raft, cut up, and floated away. It took five years to work their way through this mass, but Shreve's men finally made it. Even

The owners of steamboats took great pride in their vessels and decorated them extravagantly. Often when an owner, for sentimental reasons, gave a whole succession of his boats the same name, ornaments would be passed down from one boat to another. The Natchez Indian chief and his squaw (above) graced the dining salon of more than one of Captain Tom Leathers' seven steamboats called Natchez. Owners even took pride in how their vessels sounded. The three-belled whistle at left was carried by one of a series of boats called Grey Eagle. When the three bells sounded at once, they made a chord.

then the raft kept forming again, and not until 1880 was it cleared away finally and completely. A town grew up where Shreve had his main work camp; it was named Shreveport and is now one of Louisiana's leading cities.

The remarkable growth of western river navigation owes a great deal to Captain Henry Shreve. Twenty years after the *Washington* appeared, the number of western steamboats had a greater tonnage than all the American ships in the Great Lakes and on the Atlantic Coast combined. And still they kept coming. By 1849 there were approximately one thousand steamboats in operation on the western waters, and boat yards could not keep up with the demand.

Most steamboats were built on the Ohio and on its two tributaries, the Allegheny and the Monongahela, which join at Pittsburgh to form it. Builders sometimes even worked at night by torchlight. Steamboating was a business where the risks were great but profits were worth them. A boat on the western rivers did not last long; its average life was said to be about five years. If it was not stabbed in the vitals by a snag or blown to glory by its own boilers it would probably catch fire and burn. Often an owner who had lost a boat would be in touch with the boat yards before another day had passed, ordering a new one. A boat could pay for itself in twenty weeks.

Almost all steamboats followed the same general engine-on-a-raft design, although with many elaborations. The main deck carried the machinery with the boilers forward and the engines between the two great paddle wheels. Some had a single stern paddle wheel, but most big Mississippi boats used side wheels for better maneuverability. The main deck also contained the boat's kitchens, accommodations (if they could be dignified with such a term) for deck passengers, and space for freight. The next deck up, called the boiler deck, held passengers' staterooms, barroom, the main dining cabin, and boat's offices. A promenade ran around the outside of the staterooms, like a veranda.

The third deck was called the hurricane deck, and on it was a small group of cabins, called the texas, for the boat's officers. It got its name because passenger cabins at first were named after states—staterooms—while the texas above was something added, just as Texas had been added to the Union in 1845. On top of the texas was the pilothouse, where the best view could be had of the river. Ahead of the texas, and on each side, were the two tall, black smokestacks.

Because a steamboat had to draw as little water as possible, its towering upper works were necessarily made of thin, light material—pretty, but very flimsy. If a steamboat caught fire—and they did time after time—it blazed from stem to stern in a matter of minutes, like the pile of tinder it was. But any beautiful lady has her weaknesses, and the steamboat was certainly the beauty of the western rivers. In some

Transactions of the Institution of Naval Architects, 1861

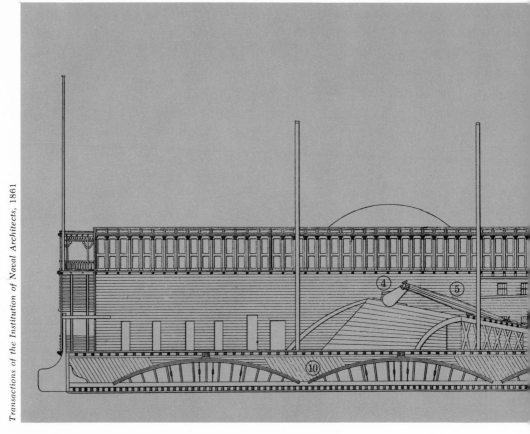

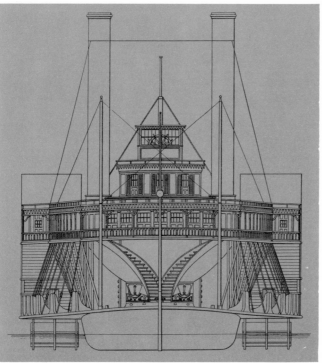

These 1861 drawings shou
typical western steamboat. Str
tural features are numbered
the cutaway view above. T
main deck (1) carries cargo a
machinery. Boilers and furna
(2) are forward; the two
gines (3) lie side by side betwe
the paddle wheels, linked to t
crankshafts (4) by connecti
rods (5). On the boiler deck
are the main cabins and sta
rooms. The hurricane deck
supports the texas (8); atop t
is the pilothouse (9). The f
arched bulkheads (10) in the h
bear the weight of the main de
The bow view (left) shows
size of the superstructure as co
pared to the shallow hull, a
the maze of struts and bra
supporting the wide main de

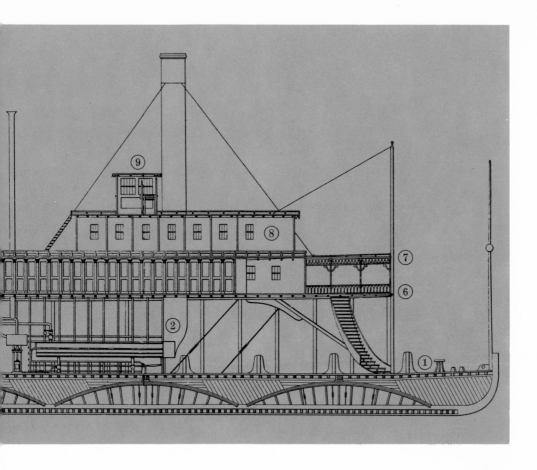

ways she was like a swan gliding over the water—tall, white, and proud.

An owner crowded as much intricate wooden scrollwork as he could afford onto his vessel, and it was sometimes said that a river steamboat looked like a wedding cake. Even the pilothouse had a crown of fancy woodwork, and sometimes its roof rose up into a dome or rounded spire that looked as though it belonged more in the Orient than in the American West. Even the tops of the tall smokestacks were flared out and cut to look like a crown of plumes, and many boats carried some emblem hung between them: a star or crescent, an outline of

a top hat, or perhaps a bale of cotton.

Steamboats were usually painted white, with some red or blue trim here and there, except for the paddle boxes covering the big side wheels, and on this large flat space the builder usually let the painter have his head. A sunburst was a favorite because it fitted perfectly into the half-circle of the paddle-wheel covering, and it permitted the use of a great many bright colors. But many other subjects were used. The *Minnesota Belle* had a well-fed, pink-cheeked young lady carrying a sheaf of grain and a sickle; the *Ben Franklin* showed Franklin flying his kite and drawing lightning from the clouds; the *Niagara,* naturally enough, displayed Niagara Falls. The boat's name was also painted on the paddle boxes, sometimes in gold leaf. Later, the craze for artwork passed, and side-wheelers bore only the name of the boat and the line that owned it.

A crack steamboat was just as ornate inside as out. The main cabin extending through the center of the second or boiler deck had its ceiling and walls cut up into just as much curlicued scrollwork as the outside of the boat. It might be painted white, or on some floating palaces it was expensively paneled in walnut and rosewood. Crystal chandeliers were common; carpets were thick and costly.

Doors opened from the main cabin into the passengers' staterooms on either side. Usually each stateroom door bore a painting, although, since both artistic taste and talent were scarce in the West, they were usually pretty bad. Some boats boasted sumptuous furnishings—French mirrors with hand-carved frames, upholstered chairs, and marble-topped tables in the ladies' cabins. The *J. M. White* outdid her rivals by having double beds instead of bunks.

The *Eclipse,* a steamboat of the early 1850's, and one of the largest ever to sail the Mississippi, was 365 feet long and had paddle wheels 41 feet in diameter; by comparison, a football field is 300 feet long, and 41 feet is just about the height of a four-

story building. There were 121 in her crew, and she carried 180 passengers (not including deck passengers, who did not count), and forty-eight of her staterooms were of sufficient magnificence to be advertised as bridal suites.

The *J. M. White* was one of the truly famous boats of the river, and despite the double beds, her reputation was based more on speed than on luxury. The *White* was built in 1844, and was designed by a man named William King. Knowing that the bow wave turned up by a moving steamboat

The Mayflower, *shown here in a Currier and Ives print of 1855, was one of the most elegant and handsome steamboats on the river. She made the St. Louis-New Orleans run.*

dipped, then rose again to a second crest, King designed his boat so that the paddle wheels would bite deeply into this second swell of water. At first the builder refused to go ahead because King's plan would put the wheels twenty feet farther aft than they were on any other boat, and he was sure it would ruin the vessel. But in the end Billy King got his way.

The *J. M. White* turned out to be the fastest craft on the river. In her first season she made the run from New Orleans to St. Louis in three days, twenty-three hours and nine minutes —a record that was not bettered until 1870 when the *Robert E. Lee* cut almost five hours from that time. But old steamboatmen pointed out that the

river had made several cutoffs during those years, shortening itself by many miles; many insisted the *J. M. White* was the fastest side-wheeler of all time.

Other steamboatmen tried to hire Billy King to design them a boat even faster than the *White*. But he only shook his head and said that if ever a boat came along that would beat the *J. M. White*'s time, then he would make one to go even faster. He never had to do it in his lifetime.

The *Eclipse* and the *J. M. White* and the *Robert E. Lee* were grand and famous boats, but there were hundreds and hundreds of others, plain little hard-working packets, most of them forever forgotten, which plied the Mississippi and many of its branches. A packet was a steamboat that carried passengers and mail as well as freight on a regular schedule, as distinguished from towboats.

Little streams that do not look today as though they could be depended upon to float a cigar box except after a long rainy spell not only saw steamboats but had regular packet service. The craft that ran on them were designed to get along practically without water. Rivermen said they could travel across a meadow on a heavy dew, and that in low water the captain could open a keg of beer and travel for miles on the foam. The *Iowa City* drew only twenty inches of water, and the *Chippewa Falls* only twelve when not loaded; both boats operated on tributaries of the upper Mississippi.

Tall tales were told about some of these little boats. The *Monitor*, it was said, ran aground in the Chippewa River in Wisconsin one day in 1863; a short time later she floated free without any trouble. Accounts have it that she had gone aground on her starboard side but had come free the moment the pilot shifted his quid of tobacco from the starboard to the port side of his jaw. It was also claimed that when the *Monitor* ran onto a bar, a deck hand would get out on each side and the two would lift her over.

It did not take long for the steamboat to open the far and wild places of the Mississippi Valley. The upper Mississippi had been penetrated quite early. In 1818 a low-pressure boat managed to go as far above the mouth of the Ohio as Kaskaskia, Illinois, but she was a quite ineffective craft, and it was not much of a trip. But in the spring of 1823 a real steamboat, the *Virginia*, headed north. She passed between high rock bluffs where there were only Indians to watch her; the only craft that shared the river with her were canoes and bateaux belonging to fur traders.

On May 10, the *Virginia*'s whistle echoed from the bluff on which the lonely northern army outpost of Fort Snelling stood. The head of navigation, the Falls of St. Anthony, was only eight or ten miles farther upstream. That first steamboat was soon followed by others; within a short time the traffic on the upper river was a flood, and towns and farms were springing up along the streams.

The main cabin of the Grand Republic, *with its thick carpets, massive gas chandeliers, and gingerbread woodwork, was the most grandiose cabin on the Mississippi in the 1880's.*

Boats also began puffing up the muddy and treacherous Missouri very early. The first was the *Independence,* which in 1819 ran to the mouth of the Chariton River, about two thirds of the way across Missouri. Each year boats went a little farther until, in 1860, Fort Benton in Montana was reached—2,200 miles up the river. This was as far as they ever ran regularly, although occasionally boats got a little farther in times of high water.

Missouri River steamboating had its own problems because the river was so changeable, so choked with sand bars, so wild in floodtime, and so very low in periods of dry weather. The stern-wheeler was soon adopted on the Missouri because in times of low water the channel was not much wider in places than the boat, and side wheels would have made the boat too wide in a tight spot.

The boats also carried special equipment which, while also used on the Mississippi in emergencies, was an absolute necessity on the Missouri. When a boat ran into trouble on a bar, long wooden spars were stood in the water at a slant, one on each side of the boat, looking a little like the legs of a grasshopper. Lines and hoists were attached

When this fine lithograph was made in 1849, Pittsburgh had become a thriving, bustling city, its docks crowded with steamboats. The city was known as the "Gateway to the West" because of the number of settlers who started their westward journeys by boarding Ohio River boats here.

over the tops of the spars, power was applied through a steam capstan, and the boat half-lifted, half-pushed itself off the bar. This operation, called sparring off, was often the only way a boat could proceed.

Settlers liked the lower Missouri, but for a long time the only boat traffic on the upper river was limited almost entirely to hunters, trappers, and the United States Army. This was country of the Sioux, Crow, and other such tribes who believed that the only good

white man was a dead one. As often as not, the stern-wheelers fought battles with Indians who fired at them from the banks, then raced across necks of land to be waiting again when the boat had made the long trip around the bend. No wonder that iron plating on the pilothouse was standard equipment. Eventually, even steamboating on the Missouri became almost routine, but for a long time it was quite different from the kind of steamboating that Mark Twain wrote about.

5. Lords of the River

Anyone connected with a steamboat was touched by glory. A Negro roustabout on the lower river before the Civil War was usually a free man and felt he had every reason to strut and lord it over his brethren ashore who labored in slavery. And if working on a steamboat could glorify even these lowly, hard-working people, it made the captain and the pilot without any doubt the absolute lords of all creation.

A captain not only commanded his boat, but the chances were that he also owned it. In the East, companies usually owned the boats and employed captains to operate them, but westerners were independent men who liked to be their own bosses. A good captain knew everything that was going on aboard his boat. He kept a check on the engine room machinery and on the chief engineer's fuel and oil bills. He watched what food was being taken aboard and made sure it was being cooked and served correctly so that his passengers would praise his table and travel with him on their next trip. He had to be on friendly terms with shippers in order to persuade them to send their cotton or corn or crockery on his boat.

The captain was an absolute autocrat in everything except matters pertaining to the navigation of the boat; there the pilot was supreme. He could, and sometimes did, drop a passenger

The wheelhouse of an old Mississippi steamboat, shown in this photograph, was equipped with high chairs that gave the pilot, captain, and other officers a clear view of the river. The 1887 woodcut on the opposite page includes the captain, mate, and clerk of the steamer Alvin.

off on a lonely, muddy stretch of riverbank for not much more reason than that he did not like his looks.

When stories were told about famous captains, "Roaring Jack" Russell's name was always one that came up. Russell was a man from Kentucky, big and tough and incredibly strong, who had begun his career shortly after 1800 as a flatboatman, becoming familiar with the moods and dangers of the rivers by floating down the Kentucky and Ohio and Mississippi to New Orleans. Tales are told of how he whipped a New Orleans bully who taunted rivermen and made Kentuckians his special target; no one else had been able to stand up against him until Jack Russell thrashed him in a battle that men talked of for years after.

Russell loved to dance. Once, at a dance in New Orleans, a very flashily dressed man with many rings and other jewelry tripped him. Russell thought it an accident, but when it happened a second time and he saw it had been done on purpose, he knocked the man flat. The man was Jean Lafitte, the pirate, a person not accustomed to being knocked down. He left and soon returned with his crew; a noisy gun battle followed between the boatmen barricaded inside the building and the pirates outside, but militia broke it up before too much damage had been done.

Russell fought in the War of 1812 and then returned to flatboating, but the first steamboats were puffing over the water, and he soon went to work on the new craft. Many stories were told of his courage during explosions, fires, and collisions, and his strength was tremendous. Once he supposedly carried a load weighing 1,245 pounds from one side of a steamboat deck to the other, and he was said to have lifted a weight of 1,647 pounds.

At one time Captain Russell's *Constellation* tied up for the night at the wide-open, roaring, boisterous river port of Natchez-under-the-Hill, and some of his passengers went ashore to see the notorious gambling and drinking houses. One man was robbed of his pocketbook, and when Captain Russell heard the story the next morning, he agreed to do what he could.

He went to the gambling house and demanded the pocketbook back, only to be met with a chorus of guffaws from the den of thieves. Captain Russell quietly announced that he would give them until the departure time of his boat to produce the pocketbook and the money. When that time came, he asked once more and was answered with curses. Thereupon he had his deck hands wrap a stout cable around the house and make the other end fast to the *Constellation*. He gave the order for the boat to move ahead slowly. The cable tightened, the house started to creak and crack and then to tilt a little. Captain Russell won: the ruffians yelled to him to stop, and the pocketbook, with all the money still in it, was handed over at once.

Then there was Captain Tom Leathers, a giant of a man, 6 feet 4 inches,

and weighing 270 pounds. Leathers had a love affair with the city of Natchez, Mississippi; he came from Kentucky, but after he had settled in Natchez it was the one place on earth he wanted to live. He built and commanded seven steamboats during his stay there, and there was only one possible name for them; each one, as it came along, was christened *Natchez.* He loved each one and spared nothing to try to make them the most luxurious boats on the river. His fifth boat cost $200,000; he paid $5,000 for the carpets alone, a fantastic figure in that day. Of his seven *Natchez*es, four were burned, two were ripped by snags, and one was captured by Union troops during the Civil War. Steamboats seldom died of old age.

Captain Tom was a man who knew how to attract attention. On the river,

In this 1862 lithograph, Captain Leathers' fifth steamboat named Natchez *surges ahead, a Confederate naval ensign snapping in the wind. The* Natchez *was burned in 1863 while being used in a Confederate naval campaign.*

he liked to cut across another boat's bow, forcing it to give way in a tight spot. It left the captain of the other vessel cursing, but it made people talk about Captain Leathers, and that brought him business. It is said that he had a command of profanity never equaled on the river; he could start on some unhappy victim, and in a masterpiece of swearing, without repeating himself, make the subject of his attentions shrivel up completely. Once, when someone took him to task for his cursing, he is supposed to have answered, "What's the use of being a steamboat captain if you can't tell the world to go to the devil?"

Only one person could handle Captain Tom. His wife was a little lady of about a hundred pounds, and whenever she thought his roaring had gone far enough, she needed only to say, "Now, Tom," and her giant of a husband would calm down. He died on his eightieth birthday, struck down in New Orleans by a hit-and-run bicyclist.

Captain Joseph LaBarge did his steamboating on the Missouri, and was not only owner and captain of his boats, but pilot as well. More than once he had to hold off Indians as his boat made its way along the crooked river; one time the Sioux followed him for six hundred miles from Fort Pierre to Fort Union, shooting at him every chance they got. At one place where the channel swung right over against a high bank he had to use a cannon to drive off the Indians.

In the big flood of 1844 he took his *Nimrod* down to St. Louis along a river whose channel was completely altered in a world of rushing water which spread for miles and hid every landmark. When he finally reached St. Louis and found the levee under water, he ran the *Nimrod* up the street and tied her directly to the warehouse. Another time, when a tornado played roughly with the upper works of his boat, Captain LaBarge made a new roof for his pilothouse from buffalo hide and used cylinders of the same material, dried and hard, to replace his smokestacks that had blown away. On the Missouri, there were no convenient boat yards to repair a damaged vessel; a captain did what he could.

In addition to the captain, the other supreme being aboard a steamboat was the pilot—or, rather, the pilots, because there had to be at least two of them to stand watches. If a captain had to know everything that went on aboard a steamboat, a pilot had to have exact knowledge of the river and how to take a boat through it. He might not know how to wind a clock on the boat, but on the river he had to be acquainted with every snag, bar, rock, caving bank, and bend, and to know what happened to the channel when the river rose five feet or when it dropped ten.

No one has written so well about piloting as Mark Twain in *Life on the Mississippi*. Of course, Twain stretched the truth in telling of his months as a cub or apprentice to pilot Horace Bixby; he always did, if it made a good story better. He was not quite so young nor so ignorant of what piloting involved as he would have his readers believe. But he was not being disrespectful of the truth in telling all that had to be learned by a young man who wanted to become a pilot.

Mr. Bixby, besides teaching him to handle steamboats, at once set out to "learn him the river." He started by naming off every town, point, bend, island, and bar which the boat passed between New Orleans and St. Louis, and his cub jotted all the names down in a notebook. But he found they were all in the book and not in his head.

He was further discouraged when he realized that, since he and Mr. Bixby had been on watch only four hours out of every eight, he had only half the river set down. Another blow came after they left St. Louis and started back downriver again; the river looked completely different going down than coming up; he would have to learn it *both* ways. And still another thing helped to break his heart as he listened to visiting pilots as they sat on the bench provided for them in the pilot-house and talked shop:

"'Jim, [one said] how did you run Plum Point, coming up?'

"'It was in the night, there, and I ran it the way one of the boys on the *Diana* told me; started out about fifty yards above the wood pile on the false point, and held on the cabin under Plum Point till I raised the reef—quarter less twain—then straightened up for the middle bar till I got well abreast the old one-limbed cotton-wood in the bend, then got my stern on the cotton-wood and head on the low place above the point, and came through a-booming—nine and a half.'

"'Pretty square crossing, an't it?'

"'Yes, but the upper bar's working down fast.'"

As they went on talking, the cub realized that he not only had to know the names of all the towns and islands and bends, "but I must even get up a

Captain Thomas P. Leathers, a fiery giant of a man, looked every inch a keen-eyed river boat skipper when he posed for this photograph. Captain Leathers' aggressive way of forcing his boats ahead of other craft on the Mississippi won him the extremely appropriate nickname, "Old Push."

Hannibal, Missouri—the scene of Mark Twain's boyhood—is shown in the painting above, looking down the Mississippi, and on the opposite page, looking upriver. The island on the horizon of the downriver view was Huck Finn's and Tom Sawyer's hide-out.

warm personal acquaintanceship with every old snag and one-limbed cottonwood and obscure wood pile that ornaments the banks of this river for twelve hundred miles; and more than that, I must actually know where these things are in the dark. . . ."

Every time the cub began to think he was making headway, Mr. Bixby would bring up something else. One time it was to ask the shape of Walnut Bend. He exploded when his cub said he did not know, but calmed down and explained that a pilot had to know the shape of the entire river perfectly, better than he knew the hallway in his own home, because on a dark night all he had left to steer by was the shape in his head. Otherwise, said Mr. Bixby, he would take shadows on the water for the bank, and would steer where he should not, but if he knew the shape perfectly, he would pay no attention to what he thought he saw.

The cub also discovered he was not done when he had learned the river once. Banks caved, bars formed or shifted position, snags took up residence in the channel, and the channel itself shifted about in the bed of the river, so that the process of learning never ended.

As if all these things were not enough, the cub had to learn to "read the river." The surface of the river told a pilot a great many things about what went on below. A certain type of long, slanting line meant that there was a bluff reef below—a bar with steep sides not far below the surface. A kind of dimple on the water warned that there was a hulk or a rock waiting to wreck a careless pilot's boat. Tumbling, boiling rings said that a bar was dissolving and the channel changing, while a slick spot with circles and radiating lines proclaimed that the bot-

tom there was building up and becoming dangerously shallow. And, as the cub learned to his great embarrassment, a breeze could cause a "wind reef" that looked exactly like the danger signal of a bluff reef. Mr. Bixby could not explain to his cub how one told them apart. "By and by you will just naturally *know* one from the other, but you never will be able to explain why or how you know them apart."

When his cub had begun to learn some of these bewildering lessons, Mr. Bixby brought him down to earth once again by pointing out that a steamboat could go places at high water that it could not go at other times, that a pilot must be constantly alert to know whether the river is rising or falling, and that he must have many hundreds or thousands of personal little signposts, such as a certain stump which would indicate to him, when the water reached its roots, that a certain chute still many miles upstream (a chute is the passage behind an island) then

had enough water in it to carry a steamboat through safely. And the cub, once again overcome by all he still had to learn, asked whether there were many of these chutes.

"I should say so [Mr. Bixby answered]. I fancy we shan't run any of the river this trip as you've ever seen it run before—so to speak. If the river begins to rise again, we'll go up behind bars that you've always seen standing out of the river, high and dry like the roof of a house; we'll cut across low places that you've never noticed at all, right through the middle of bars that cover three hundred acres of river; we'll creep through cracks where you've always thought was solid land; we'll dart through the woods and leave twenty-five miles of river off to one side; we'll see the hind-side of every island between New Orleans and Cairo."

But Samuel Clemens did learn the river during eighteen months as Horace Bixby's cub, and went on to serve

73

for several happy years as a pilot in his own right. Then the Civil War came and drove the graceful white boats from the river, and Sam drifted out west to the mining camps, and then became a writer. When he looked about for a pen name, he remembered his days on the river and the cry of the leadsman taking soundings in a shallow stretch of channel. Depth was measured in fathoms, a fathom being six feet. "Mark three" meant three fathoms, or eighteen feet. "Quarter-less-three" meant one quarter of a fathom less than three full fathoms, or sixteen and a half feet. "Half twain" was two and a half fathoms, or fifteen feet, and "mark twain" was an even two fathoms. Mark Twain had the right sound, and it was the name Samuel Clemens adopted. It was a good name for a man who had grown up on the river and had worked on it and loved it.

These cartoons, dating from 1858, poke fun at the hazards involved in western steamboating. From left to right: a steamboat plummets down the Falls of the Ohio; another one runs aground; and a third is impaled on a sawyer.

As soon as a steamboat had backed away from the wharf, the pilot was in complete command of navigating her. If he decided the boat should tie up for the night, she was tied up. If he was driving the vessel into what the captain was sure was certain destruction, the captain could do nothing; in fact, the law forbade him to interfere in any way with the pilot.

As befitted a man of such power in such a difficult profession, he received princely pay. A list of average wages in 1857 on the upper Mississippi showed captains getting $300 a month while the two pilots on a boat received $500 each. And in 1866, a captain on the Missouri got only $200 a month while the pilots drew $1,200. And this in a day when $400 a month was an income far beyond the dreams of most men. When Mark Twain came back to visit the river in 1882, he considered it a measure of the way the pilot had fallen from his former grand station in life that the captain's salary had by then been raised higher than the pilot's.

Of course, a pilot on the Missouri deserved more than other pilots. On

. ALL: *Harper's Magazine*, 1858

that restless river, with its heavy load of silt, sand bars could form or disappear overnight, whole acres of banks caved into the stream, and cutoffs were frequent. Under those conditions, a pilot could learn the river only in a general way because the channel he followed on one trip would be completely changed by the time of his next trip. He had to depend very much on instinct, knowing from the eddy and flow of the currents what lay beneath.

Besides all the other hazards of the Missouri, it was a terror for snags. The everlasting caving of its banks dropped so many of these steamboat killers into the river that in places they made the channel almost impassable. Figures tell the story: up to 1894, 294 steamboats were recorded as having been lost on the Missouri, and 193 of these—very nearly two thirds—were victims of snags.

In all ways but one it was a more difficult stream to navigate than the Mississippi. That one exception was night navigation. The muddy Missouri looked whitish at night and was much easier for a pilot to read than the Mis-

This photograph of Samuel Clemens, better known as Mark Twain, was taken in 1873.

sissippi, which was black and told him nothing.

But Mississippi or Missouri, Arkansas or Red, Yazoo or St. Croix, Wabash or Rock, they all had their problems and their pleasures. One can be sure that even on quiet little streams like the Chippewa or the Maquoketa, there were a great many glorious summer mornings when a young pilot would glance at the leafy banks so close on either side he could almost spit to them, look around the cramped pilothouse of his miniature packet steamer, and then decide, as he steadied the wheel, that there was nothing in the world—absolutely nothing—that he would rather be doing.

All the commotion and clatter of the New Orleans levee near sailing time is captured in this 1883 painting of steamboats being loaded with a wide variety of cargo for the journey upriver.

6. Steamboat Comin'

The pilot and the captain might be the most glamorous figures aboard a big packet, but the vessel could not have moved an inch if it had to depend on them alone. It took a good-sized crew to operate a large steamboat. There were engineers and there were firemen to stoke the furnaces, there were roustabouts to handle the freight, there were deck hands, and on the floating palaces there were whole platoons of cooks and stewards to wait on tables, maids to make beds and take care of the cabins, a bartender or two, a barber, and possibly even a band if the boat was grand enough.

77

The engine-room crew lived in a world of their own, one of great, moving machinery and hissing steam and red glare from the furnace doors on the dark, sweating bodies of firemen. The passengers taking the air up on the hurricane deck might admire the confident man in the pilothouse, but it was the greasy men below who kept the big paddle wheels turning. As many as ten boilers supplied high-pressure steam to the two engines—there were always two in a side-wheeler, one connected to each paddle wheel. It was thus possible to operate the wheels independently, even to have one wheel go ahead while the other was in reverse. This made the side-wheeler very maneuverable, but it also meant that the engineers had to be constantly alert, ready to respond instantly to orders from the pilothouse of "Stop the starboard! Stop the larboard. Ahead easy on the larboard."

Not all engineers were capable men. Some steamboat owners, knowing that the average life of their boats, in the face of boiler explosions, fires, and snags, was only four or five years, built them cheaply, put in second-rate engines, and hired incompetent engi-

To keep steamboats steaming, stokers were required to perform the unending, backbreaking task of feeding pieces of wood (or, in this case, shoveling coal) into the red-hot iron furnaces that heated the boat's huge boilers.

Every Saturday, 1871

neers who would work for poor wages. But there were also a great many capable men in the engine rooms who had a sense of dedication to their work. When, in 1847, the *Talisman* was rammed by another boat off Cape Girardeau, Missouri, engineer Butler stuck by his engines as the pilot tried to bring the boat to the bank. When the water reached Butler's waist, the captain ordered him to abandon ship, but he refused and died at his post.

And, of course, there was Jim Bludso of the *Prairie Belle* about whom a ballad was composed:

> He weren't no saint—them engineers
> Is pretty much all alike—
> One wife in Natchez-under-the-Hill
> And another one here in Pike.

As always happens in such cases, a lot of pure imagination and fancy got mixed up with the facts, but the central truth is there. The *Prairie Belle* caught fire off the town of Louisiana, Missouri, and the pilot drove her to the bank. But in order to hold her there while the passengers got ashore, the wheels had to be kept turning, and Jim Bludso, in the engine room, kept them moving, giving his own life to make good his promise, according to the ballad:

> I'll hold her nose agin the bank
> Till the last galoot's ashore.

The common laborers of a steamboat were the roustabouts. Their job was to load and unload the freight, and every time the boat came in for a landing and the gangplank went down, they went into action. They trotted on and off, carrying the bales of cotton or barrels of salt or crates of axes or any of the thousands of items of freight the river boats carried, and when they were on their way again, they could throw themselves down and catch their breath. It was not easy work, but they were men who would be doing hard work anyway; better to do it on a steamboat than ashore.

It was the mate who drove the roustabouts on who caught the attention of onlookers. Mark Twain has given us a description of the mate on the *Paul Jones,* the boat on which he first became a pilot's cub:

". . . He was huge and muscular, his face was bearded and whiskered all over; he had a red woman and a blue woman tattooed on his right arm—one on each side of a blue anchor with a red rope to it; and in the matter of

These tired roustabouts relax after the furious activity of loading and stowing cargo.

Harper's Magazine, 1893

79

BILL OF FARE

St. Louis, Cairo, Memphis & New-Orleans Passenger Packet
M. S. MEPHAM

A. H. SHAW, Master.   JEWETT WILCOX, Clerk.

Printed in oil colors by P. S. Duval, Philad.

Breakfast from 7½ to 9 A. M.
Dinner from 1 to 2½ P. M.
Supper at 6 P. M

JAMES ABBEY Steward.

STR. "ED. RICHARDSON."

DINNER.

For _____ 1879

SOUP.

FISH.
Broiled Red Fish, au maitre d'hote.

BOILED.

| Leg of Mutton, Caper Sauce | | Corned Beef and Cabbage |
| Chicken, Egg Sauce | Ham | Fulton Market Beef |

ROAST.

| Loin of Beef | Pork | | Chicken |
| Saddle of Mutton | | | Turkey |

VEGETABLES.

| Mashed Potatoes | Rice | Cabbage | Hominy |
| Turnips | Snap Beans | | Green Corn |

RELISHES.

Crosse & Blackwell's Pickles

Gherkins	Currant Jelly		Cheese
Tomato Catsup	Walnut Catsup		Chow-Chow
Piccalilli	English Onions		Mushroom Catsup
The Lea & Perrin Sauces	Spanish Olives		Cold Slaugh
Maunsel White	Lettuce		John Bull's Sauce
Horse Radish			French Mustard

ENTREES.

Calves' feet a la Puceline	Pieds de Veau a la Puceline
Filets of Chicken with Truffes	Filets de Poulets aux Truffes
Braised Brisket of Lamb with Green Peas	
Poitrine d'Agneau au Brasier avec Pois Verts	

GAME.

COLD DISHES.

| Corned Beef | Tongue | Ham | Salad |

A reproduction of the menu served on the New Orleans, Natchez, Cannon was commander and T. J. Howard clerk. The passengers

PASTRY AND DESSERT.

PUDDINGS.
White Raisin, a la Windsor, Vanilla Sauce

PASTRY.

| Lemon Pie | | Green Apple Pie |
| Petite Puit d'Amour | Fachennottes, a la Flour de Orange | |

CAKES.

| Pound | Fruit | Almond | Jelly Cake |
| Lady Fingers | | Cocoanut Plarine | |

CREAMS AND JELLIES.

Jelly de Macedonia		Maraschino Jelly
Meringue aux Peche		Cream a la Roman
	Belle Fritters	

FRUITS.

Pecans	Figs		Almonds
Pine Apples			Raisins
	Brazilian Nuts		Filberts
English Walnuts			Fresh Dates
Oranges	Bananas	Apples	Prunes

——COFFEE.——

Any want of attention on the part of attendants, please report to the
STEWARD.

Vicksburg and Memphis packet, _Ed. Richardson_, of which John W. were expected to eat their way straight through.

The dinner menu above was issued to passengers aboard the steamboat Ed. Richardson *in 1879. Like so many others, this boat offered an elaborate variety of dishes. At left is the ornate cover of a menu used on the* Mepham, *a boat that once offered a selection of two dozen wines.*

profanity he was sublime. When he was getting out cargo at a landing, I was always where I could see and hear. He felt all the majesty of his great position, and made the world feel it, too. When he gave even the simplest order, he discharged it like a blast of lightning, and sent a long, reverberating peal of profanity thundering after it. I could not help contrasting the way in which the average landsman would give an order, with the mate's way of doing it. If the landsman should wish the gangplank moved a foot farther forward, he would probably say: 'James, or William, one of you push that plank forward, please;' but put the mate in his place, and he would roar out: 'Here, now, start that gangplank for'ard! Lively, now! *What*'re you about! Snatch it! *snatch* it! There! there! Aft again! Aft again! Don't you hear me? Dash it to dash! are you going to *sleep* over it! 'Vast heaving. 'Vast heaving, I tell you! Going to heave it clear astern? WHERE're you going with that barrel! *for'ard* with it 'fore I make you swallow it, you dash-dash-dash-*dashed* split between a tired mud-turtle and a crippled hearse-horse!'

"I wished I could talk like that."

The mate may have been a colorful man, but the truth was less pleasant

As this 1858 cartoon indicates, mealtime aboard one of the smaller river boats could be a wild—and even dangerous—experience.

than Twain suggests. Many mates were brutal men with little consideration for those under them, and they sometimes carried clubs and were not slow about using them. Nor was there much in the way of accommodations for roustabouts; they slept where they could and were expected to take care of themselves.

Things changed in the later years of steamboating. There were so many complaints about the actions of some steamboatmen that Congress and several states passed laws prescribing just what the various officers could and could not do. Crews were protected against brutality. The good old days were gone—but sometimes it seemed they had been good mainly for steamboat owners and officers.

For the traveler in a first-class cabin on a fine packet, a trip on the river could be very pleasant. Some of the fancier vessels had wood paneling and oil paintings and cut-glass chandeliers. Captains who ran such ships took great pains to see that favored passengers got the best of everything. Meals were usually very elaborate, with many choices of food. Woods and prairies were teeming with game, and so besides beef, pork, chicken, and other domestic meats, a passenger could eat all he wanted of items like venison, prairie chicken, passenger pigeon, wild turkey, and wild duck, as well as various kinds of fish. The menus were long; one that has come down to us lists seven soups and fifteen desserts.

Once in a while there is a faint suspicion that men and women found the steamboats grand and luxurious largely by contrast with the rough and raw surroundings to which they were accustomed. Most American towns of the Mississippi Valley of that period were, to put it mildly, stinking mudholes in wet weather and choking with dust in dry, and the gaudiness of even a second-rate packet steamboat must have seemed like pure luxury to someone from such a place. Europeans were not usually so impressed with the steamboat. Certainly Charles Dickens, the great English author who visited America in 1842, was not enchanted. He made a trip from Pittsburgh down the Ohio as far as Cincinnati, and had this to say about it:

"The *Messenger* is a high-pressure boat, carrying forty passengers, exclusive of poorer persons on the lower deck. There was no mast, cordage, tackle, or rigging, only a long, ugly roof, two towering iron chimneys, and below on the sides, the doors and windows of the staterooms; the whole supported on beams and pillars, resting on a dirty barge, but a few inches above the water's edge, and in this narrow space between the upper structure and this barge's deck are the furnace fires and machinery, open at the sides.

"Within, there is one long, narrow cabin, the whole length of the boat, from which the staterooms open on both sides, a small portion of it in the stern, partitioned off for the ladies, and the bar at the opposite extreme. There is a long table down the center, and at either end a stove."

Perhaps it is worth remembering that Dickens at this time was not feeling kindly toward the United States because his books were being reprinted here without his permission and without any payment being made to him. He had little good to say about anything in this country. But he was not the only one. Michael Chevalier, a Frenchman who was very fair in what he wrote about America, called the steamboats "floating barracks." Said he: "Excellent as these boats are, great as is the service they render America, when the first feeling of curiosity is once satisfied, a long confinement in

one of them has little that is attractive for a person of a cultivated mind and refined manners."

Dickens and Chevalier were both foreigners, but even some Americans found the steamboats less than perfect. A woman who had traveled on the *Grey Eagle*, supposedly one of the finest boats on the river, tells us that her bunk was so narrow that when she turned over at night she fell out of it and hit the washbasin on the opposite wall. She also complained that the

The elegant ladies' cabin of the J. M. White, *launched in 1878, is seen reflected in a mirror in the photograph above. The plan below shows the layout of staterooms on the boiler deck of the big steamboat* Robert E. Lee.

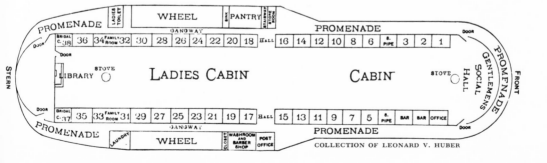

COLLECTION OF LEONARD V. HUBER

The Mississippi steamboat in the Currier and Ives print above has put in at a riverside woodyard to renew her fuel supply. Fuel might be needed any time of the day or night; wooding up at night was done by the light of bonfires and cressets—iron fire baskets like that at left, filled with burning, oil-soaked wood.

Woodcutters like the man at right, shown with his family, built flimsy cabins on the mosquito-infested banks of the rivers, hoping to sell their meager supply of wood to passing boats. The 1855 woodcut at far right shows a woodcutter bargaining with an irritated customer who is trying to beat off a cloud of mosquitos.

meals were poorly served and the general service bad. So it appears that one's impression of life on a steamboat depended partly on what boat he was on and partly on what he was used to.

With hundreds of boats cruising up and down the western rivers, tremendous amounts of fuel were used. There was coal along the Ohio, and during the later years of steamboating it was brought down into the Mississippi by barge and used by many of the packets there; but in general, cordwood was the fuel of most river boats. Just about every riverbank farmer spent part of his time chopping down trees, cutting them into four-foot lengths, and splitting them to the right size for a boat's furnaces. Then, after piling the wood on the riverbank, he would wait for a customer. The pilot would bring his vessel up to the bank, the gangplank would be lowered, and with the mate driving them on, the roustabouts would bring the wood aboard and stack it near the boilers. Wooding up at night was exciting, since it was done by the light of bonfires and torches. There were thousands of woodyards along the river; at night, when it was too dark to see them, the pilot would ring a special signal on his bell and any wood lot tender who heard would at once light a ready-laid bonfire to guide the pilot in.

During the later years of steamboating, the packets had to share the upper Mississippi with another kind of steamboat, the hard-working stern-wheel rafters or towboats. Already in the 1830's lumbermen had started their work of ruining the seemingly endless pine woods of Wisconsin and Minnesota, and logs or sweet-smelling lumber in rafts as big as fields floated down the river, guided by long sweep-oars handled by hard-drinking, hard-fighting raftsmen who could probably

Harper's Magazine, 1855

have taken Mike Fink apart into small pieces in a battle. Then the rivermen began experimenting with towboats, and in 1863 a boat named the *Union* became the first rafter. Soon every log and lumber raft that went downriver had a powerful stern-wheeler nudging it along.

Logs were made up into rafts in sloughs, the quiet-water side of an island. They were so arranged that the raft could be split lengthwise to allow the halves to be taken separately through the narrow passages between the piers of railroad bridges. Rafts varied greatly in size, but over a considerable part of the rafting days they would run about 600 feet long by 275 feet wide—about three acres. When ready, the rafter took its place behind the raft (river towboats always push their tow), the pilot rang for power on the paddle wheel, and the trip was on.

A pilot on a packet was a skilled man, but all he had to steer was the boat under him. A rafter pilot had to worry about a field of logs with stubborn ideas about where it wanted to go To guide it, cables were fastened from the stern of the towboat to the rear corners of the raft in such a way that, by loosening one line and tightening the other with a winch, the towboat was drawn at an angle to the raft, just like a big rudder. Then, as the boat strained and huffed and churned up the river, the raft would slowly swing in one direction or the other, and be headed right for the next bend.

Raftsmen on the forward corners of the raft helped steer as best they could with sweep-oars, but rivermen later lashed a second steamboat crossways at the front of the raft. Then, in answer to whistle signals from the pilot in the rear boat, the bow boat drove its paddle wheel forward or in reverse as needed, pulling the head of the raft to right or left. This made handling a raft almost a business for a sane man—to make it hard again, rafts were increased in size. During the later years of rafting, some of them reached unbelievable proportions. In 1901, the *Saturn* brought a lumber raft down the Mississippi that was 1,450 feet long by 270 feet wide. The *F. C. A. Denckman* handled one 1,625 feet by 275 feet, and the *J. W. Van Sant* once was responsible for a raft 1,400 feet by 276 feet—not quite so large in area as the previous two, but a double-decker, with the lower layer of logs running lengthwise and the upper crosswise.

Even under the best of circumstances a log raft was an ornery thing to handle, and with the current urging it on, it was impossible to stop if trouble appeared ahead. If a raft hit an island or a bar, as likely as not the river would suddenly be full of stray logs.

Captain E. E. Heerman, who was also a pilot, and one of the best on the upper river with either packet or rafter, had an experience that illustrates some of the woes of rafting. In 1874 he was taking a log raft down to Burlington, Iowa, with his own boat, the *Minnietta*, and had just reassembled the raft after splitting it to get it through the piers of a railroad bridge. He was just getting under way again when the black funnel of a tornado dropped from a low, black cloud and headed toward the raft.

The *Minnietta* was almost blown on her side, but Captain Heerman managed to bring her stern into the wind. Even so, she was blown up on the shore. As for the raft, it was shattered completely, except for one section of about forty logs, made specially strong because it was the part of the raft to which mooring cables were fastened. On it the raft crew had taken refuge and were saved. Every other one of the thousands of logs was on its own independent way.

It took the crew eight days to get the raft together again. Logs were found in farmers' fields, on islands, lodged in thickets, and, of course, floating down the river. It was necessary to pry and pull many of them out of brush and briers, and the clothing of captain and crew were torn until they were almost completely naked. When the raft was reassembled, enough clothing was collected to dress one of the crew decently, although a bit strangely, and he was sent into a nearby small town to buy clothes for the rest of the men. Finally, they were able to take the raft the rest of the way down to Burlington.

When Captain Heerman delivered his raft, it was found that only three logs had been lost!

The J. W. Van Sant *(background) and the* Lydia Van Sant *(serving as bow boat in the foreground), a well-known team of rafters, are shown here, near the turn of the century, edging half of their log tow through a swing bridge.*

7. Towns on the River

Most of the early settlements in the Mississippi Valley grew up along the rivers. In time, some prospered and became cities, but many never grew beyond the size of dusty little villages. And some disappeared when their few residents moved out—or because the river swallowed them up. There are hundreds of towns on the Great River, and many have stories to tell; those that follow are picked at random.

New Orleans was the queen of all the river towns, the great gateway city between the Mississippi Valley and the outside world. The French founded it in a near-swamp in 1718; it was turned over to Spain and back again to France before Napoleon, pinched for money, sold it to the United States in 1803 along with the rest of the vast Louisiana Territory.

But although New Orleans might now be an American city, it was hard for country boys fresh off flatboats to realize it. Having brought down their boatloads of hogs or corn or hides or barrel staves from back country farms, they gawked at the first real city they had ever seen. Here many people spoke French; instead of honest homespun, gentlemen and ladies wore elegant clothes even in the middle of the week; and restaurants served strange foods that made a farmer from up the Kentucky or Wabash suspicious.

Steamboat passengers landing at the thriving young city of Omaha, Nebraska, often stayed at the Herndon Hotel, shown in the 1860 water color at left. The hotel was situated on a bluff above the Missouri River.

The farm boys saw wealthy cotton and sugar planters, they saw nuns and priests who were unknown in most of their Protestant settlements, and they could not help noticing the pretty Creole girls on the iron lacework balconies. And for the first time, many of them saw human slaves.

New Orleans grew mightily. Flatboats continued to arrive by the thousands, and steamboats came not only down the Mississippi but from the bayous beyond the river where the trees hung heavy with Spanish moss. By 1840, New Orleans was the second greatest port in America.

It had its dark side. It was struck repeatedly by yellow fever, and hundreds died. Other diseases were common, largely as a result of the filth that lay in stagnant open sewers. No American city of that time did much about sanitation, but New Orleans was especially bad because it was so low that drainage was difficult. Because it was so low, there was bound to be trouble from the river, too, and although the levees were strengthened constantly, the Mississippi was a danger every time the water was high.

Nor was New Orleans a very quiet and sober city. One area was called the Swamp, and here the criminals and cutthroats hung out. It was also a favorite haunt of the tougher boatmen. The Swamp covered about half a dozen blocks, crowded with saloons, dance halls, and gambling dens. Buildings were rickety shacks made of rough lumber from old flatboats; in the

89

Market folks

In the early years of the nineteenth century, when these water colors were done, the people of St. Louis, New Orleans, and other older towns along the Mississippi were a colorful and varied group—often quite different from the inhabitants of the raw new frontier settlements who came downriver on flatboats and keelboats. Many of these river people were Creoles, descendants of the early French settlers of the Mississippi Valley. At top (left to right) are an Indian squaw, an elegant dandy, and a farmer driving a Creole cart. The market scene (left center) was painted in New Orleans by American architect Benjamin Latrobe. The Creole belle at lower left and the Creole woman and child next to her all lived in St. Louis.

saloons, the bars usually were no more than boards laid across a couple of kegs.

It was said that an average of half a dozen murders were committed every week in the Swamp over a good many years, although no one could possibly know because bodies were quietly dumped into the Mississippi. Robberies and holdups were so common that little attention was paid to them. As for fights, there were dozens every night. Supposedly, no law officer set foot within the Swamp in twenty years; any policeman who tried would have had little chance of coming out alive.

Natchez, Mississippi, was a river town that grew up where the bluffs rise above the river. They are two hundred feet high at this point, a strategic spot where the French built a fort which in turn passed to the British, the Spanish, and finally to the Americans. The place had one large advantage besides flood-free heights and very rich soil: it was the beginning of the Natchez Trace, that ancient route that led up into the Ohio Valley. Probably buffalo had first marked it out; Indians had used it; now, as the West grew, it was used by flatboatmen returning to their homes after a trip to New Orleans, and by settlers coming into the West. Natchez profited mightily from the traffic.

The rich cotton plantations in the region brought wealth and elegance to Natchez and made it one of the wealthiest towns in the United States.

Here were built some of the finest southern mansions of slavery days; many of them survive to delight tourists who visit Natchez each year to see these beautiful reminders of an age of vanished splendor.

Natchez had its share of people who had more money than sense. One planter provided his stable of race horses with stalls of paneled mahogany, hand-carved, with drinking troughs of marble. Silver posts and chains, and a silver name plate with the horse's name engraved on it, graced each stall. And in each was a large mirror so the beast could admire itself.

The boatmen and gamblers and other assorted river roughnecks who stopped at Natchez did not go where the rich people lived in the big mansions on top of the bluff. They stayed at the waterside near the wharf. There, between river and bluff, was a broad shelf of muddy land, on which was a community called Natchez-under-the-Hill—a place that for a while was as infamous, as infested with cutthroats, thieves, and general scum of the earth as any place on the river.

Most of Natchez-under-the-Hill was clustered on one street—Silver Street—which also happened to be part of the roadway from Natchez on the bluff down to the steamboat landing. The saloons and gambling houses and dance halls operated all night, and fights were commonplace. There was quite a contrast between this filthy, sinful, brawling spot down on the flats and Natchez on the bluff, where the aristocratic mansions stood so peacefully.

Occasionally the people on the bluff got tired of the mess below and descended with gun and rope, and Natchez-under-the-Hill would lose some of its enthusiasm for sin for a while. In 1840 nature took a hand with a tornado which did tremendous damage; then the river current swung in toward the bluffs, and the shelf on which Natchez-under-the-Hill stood became narrower and narrower. Long before steamboating died the place was only a ghost of its former evil self. Today it is gone.

Memphis, upriver in Tennessee, was another kind of town. It was well situated on the Chickasaw Bluffs, one of the high places along the Mississippi, but for a while it looked as though Memphis would die young. There were six other settlements in the general area competing for leadership, and Memphis did not appear to have any better chance than any of the others. Nor did the river help. Flatboats need shallow eddies near shore to make their landings, but the current shifted and left deep water in front of the straggling settlement. Then when steamboats, which need deep water, began to become numerous, the

The boats on the opposite page worked the rivers in the 1890's. Little more than the pilothouse of the Ouachita *(top) shows above her prodigious load of cotton. In the photograph below, roustabouts load cotton bales aboard large steamboats at New Orleans.*

current shifted again, and left some fine shallows in front of Memphis.

The town suffered at the hands of flatboatmen, who refused to pay wharfage fees and every so often, after drinking too much, decided it would be fun to wreck the town. Bears came out of the woods and wandered down the streets (if they could be called streets; they became so muddy during rainy spells that a team of oxen is said to have drowned in the main street).

One remarkable feature of early Memphis was the Nashoba colony. A woman named Frances Wright bought 2,000 acres near town to set up a co-operative colony to free slaves. She would buy slaves, bring them to Nash-oba, and put them to work. When the earnings from their labor equaled their purchase price, they were set free, and the money was used to purchase more slaves. But Miss Wright became ill, and without her guidance the colony sank into a state of brawling confu-sion. She finally gave up in 1829; the last thirty slaves were set free and taken to Haiti in the Caribbean.

The view of the gracious city of Natchez, Mississippi (left), was painted in 1822 by John James Audubon, the famous American naturalist and artist. Because of its location on high bluffs above the river, safe from floods, many rich planters built fine houses in Natchez and lived graciously—like the well-dressed people in the foreground of Audubon's painting. Life in the roisterous, brawling port of Natchez-under-the-Hill, shown in the woodcut below, was far from gracious, however. The denizens of this rough community were a plague to the better citizens on the bluff.

Scribner's, 1874

95

Gradually Memphis outgrew its dirty, muddy, lawless early days to become a major river port and the chief cotton market of the country. Its most terrible trials came not during the Civil War but in the dozen years following. Three times during that period, yellow fever struck, and people died faster than they could be buried. Those residents who could fled, carrying the disease to other places, but soon the city was quarantined and practically cut off from the rest of the country until the epidemic ended.

There were all sorts of river towns. There were the bustling ones, like St. Paul near the head of navigation, and St. Louis where just before the Civil War over three thousand steamboats were arriving and departing in a year, so that crowding at the levee was such that boats were sometimes tied up three deep. And there were small hamlets where weeks might go by between the rare occasions when a boat would put in for a brief moment to land or pick up a passenger or some freight, and give the citizens something to talk about for hours. But big or little, the towns had one thing in common: there was always the chocolate-colored river rolling by endlessly.

It was hard fate for a prosperous river town to have the channel change and to find itself far out of reach of the steamboats. Then, as like as not, it dwindled to a sleepy village whose main occupation was supplying nearby farmers with chewing tobacco or a piece of mule harness.

Vicksburg, the great Confederate fortress blocking the Mississippi dur-

ing half the Civil War, also found itself in trouble because of a cutoff. In
1876 the river broke across a curve,
leaving the city three miles from the
channel. But Vicksburg was important
enough to do something about. The
Yazoo River emptied into the Mississippi a few miles above Vicksburg;
Army engineers diverted the lower
part of its course into the old channel
of the Mississippi and so made the
Yazoo flow past Vicksburg. Once more
steamboats could reach the Vicksburg
water front—only now they had to go
up the Yazoo to do so!

Napoleon, Arkansas, was only one of
many towns that were nibbled to death
by the Mississippi. Another that suffered the same fate, and one much better known in history, was Kaskaskia,
Illinois. Originally an Indian village,

it became a French outpost even before the French came to New Orleans.
During the Revolution, George Rogers
Clark captured it from the British. It
was the territorial capital of Illinois
and for a while, the state capital. A
town with a fine past—but Kaskaskia
happened to be located within the
point where the Kaskaskia River joins
the Mississippi in a sharp V. The Mississippi started chewing at its east
bank, above Kaskaskia, gradually cutting across toward the other river. The
government tried to restrain it, but the
big spring floods of 1881 tore out all
their pilings and other works, and the
Mississippi broke into the smaller river.

Its new course was widened in a
hurry, and Kaskaskia became an island.
As the Mississippi worked away on its
new channel, the historic town gradu-

*The remarkably clear daguerreotype, left, shows in fine detail the
prosperous Ohio River port of Cincinnati as it appeared in 1848.*

*Bale upon bale of cotton in the wash drawing below await ship-
ment at a cotton depot near Memphis during the Civil War.*

M. & M. KAROLIK COLLECTION, BOSTON MUSEUM OF FINE ARTS

97

ally disappeared, a house or two at a time. As late as 1906 a chimney was left, but that, too, is now long gone.

Winona, Minnesota—a town that might have ceased to exist—is very much on the map today. It was founded in 1851 by Captain Orren Smith of the *Nominee,* who was having a little trouble getting wood for his boat. There were still empty stretches on the upper river at that time, without riverbank farmers to cut cordwood and have it stacked, ready to sell to passing steamboats. Captain Smith reasoned that if he could establish a river port, some of its citizens would cut cordwood for extra money. It worked out just that way for several years, and Winona prospered and grew. Then the river opened a second channel near the opposite shore, and steamboats began avoiding the Winona landing, mainly, it appears, because it had been founded by a competitor.

That could have meant a quick end

to Winona as a river port, and the men of the town called a meeting to discuss the situation. Curiously, the only announcement they made after the meeting was that they had decided to build a big courthouse; nothing was said about the vital matter of the steamboats. A crew of men went across the river and spent some weeks quarrying limestone for the courthouse from the Wisconsin bluffs and loading it onto a barge. Then when the first load was being taken back there was a terrible "accident"—it sank and blocked the new channel. Steamboats had to resume taking the channel that led by Winona and making stops at its landing. When that happened there was no further need for the people of Winona to get more limestone for the courthouse.

Then there was the river town that was not a town at all. In 1852, the agent on the *Dr. Franklin* was puzzled when a man came aboard at Galena,

Despite the ever-increasing use of steamboats on the western rivers, some of the older methods of river transportation lingered on. The log raft shown floating down the Mississippi in the 1867 painting above has arrived at Winona, Minnesota, having traveled all the way from the lumber country along the Chippewa River in Wisconsin. The flatboat was still competing with the steamboat on the Mississippi in 1838 when the view of Cairo, Illinois (below), was painted.

Eugene Robinson's Floating Palaces, Museum, Menagerie, Aquarium, and Grand Opera House, photographed at right in 1893, was a complete entertainment center on barges, towed by a steamboat. Unfortunately, despite its amazing range of entertainment, this gaudy showboat proved a financial failure.

The America, shown in the striking old photograph below taking on cargo at a cotton depot, belonged to the Cooley family, a dynasty of Mississippi steamboat owners whose many vessels plied the rivers throughout the great days of steamboating. The Ouachita, another Cooley boat, is shown on page 93.

This lovely view of St. Louis, seen from the opposite bank of the Mississippi, is one of the earliest paintings of the city. It is the work of the French artist Leon Pomarede, and dates from 1832. The steam ferry in the foreground was used to carry both cattle and passengers.

Illinois, and asked for a ticket to Rollingstone, upriver in Minnesota Territory. The man refused to believe that there was no such place and produced a large and fancy map showing a splendid community of many houses, stores, parks, theaters, churches, river landings—everything. He said he was the advance agent of about four hundred easterners now on their way; all had bought land in this beautiful paradise in the West. Pilot and captain, who knew every crook in the river, guessed it might be a spot about five miles from the new little settlement of Winona, but there was no beautiful city there; there was nothing there at all.

Very soon, on other boats, the four hundred settlers arrived—men, women, and children expecting to find the perfect city waiting. Even when they saw the empty riverbank, most still insisted on being put ashore with their belongings. They were mainly bookkeepers, clerks, salesmen, and other city dwellers who had no idea how to live on a frontier, and they suffered greatly. Some dug caves in the riverbank; others put together makeshift shelters. Many sickened and died, and when the hard northern winter began to settle in, the last of them gave up. Some settled in Winona, some managed to get back east where, one hopes, they caught the men who had swindled them so cruelly. As for Rollingstone, only its general location is known; the exact site of the riverbank caves, the miserable lean-tos, and the sad rows of graves has been long lost.

8. Cutthroats and Scoundrels

The western rivers had their share, and more, of various kinds of bad men and villainous characters. This, of course, is the story of all frontier country. Lawless men head for a land where there is no law—and there was not much law along the lower Ohio River just before the turn of the nineteenth century.

The river became a wonderful hunting ground for those who had had to leave more civilized country to save their necks. Victims were no trouble to find; they came floating by. Before long the area came to have one of the choicest collections of footpads, murderers, boat wreckers, pirates, and outlaws that has ever infested any part of this country. One of their favorite

hangouts was a place called Cave-in-Rock, a large cavern in the limestone cliff on the north side of the river in what is now Illinois. From there they could conveniently prey on boats that passed their front door, or try their gentle arts on those traveling by land, for settlers were moving to the area.

In the late 1790's a man named Wilson went into business at Cave-in-Rock, putting up a crudely lettered sign announcing to boatmen that here was "Wilson's Liquor Vault and House for Entertainment." The boatmen who

In the late nineteenth century, river boat gamblers were often cast as villains in adventure stories about the Mississippi, like the 1893 example at right. The equipment of a real gambler is at the top of the page.

BEADLE'S HALF DIME Library

Second Class Matter at the New York, N. Y., Post Office.   Copyrighted 1893, by BEADLE AND ADAMS.   September 19, 1893.

3. $2.50 a Year.   PUBLISHED WEEKLY BY BEADLE AND ADAMS.   Price, 5 cents.   Vol. XXXIII.
No. 98 WILLIAM STREET, NEW YORK.

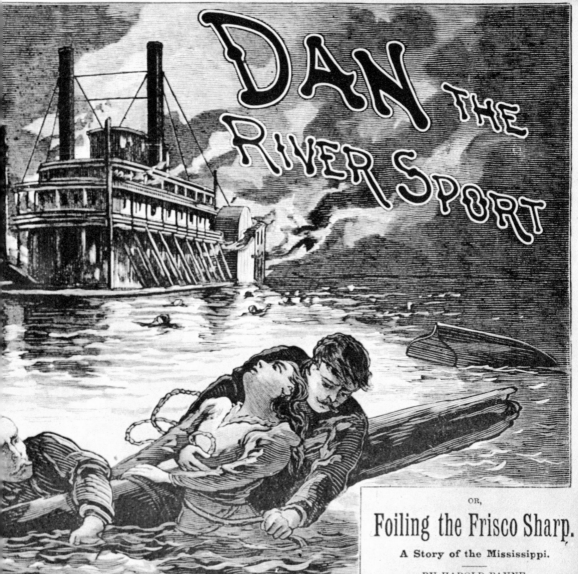

DAN THE RIVER SPORT

OR,

Foiling the Frisco Sharp.

A Story of the Mississippi.

BY HAROLD PAYNE.

CHAPTER I.

A FULL HAND.

"Excuse me, gentlemen. I have something to say in this little game! Just make her fast and shove out that gang-plank again, or some of you will be putting your families to the expense of buyin' crape in about a second!"

"WILL LASH YOU TO THE SPAR WITH THIS ROPE, AND DO WHAT I CAN TO PADDLE IT ASHORE."

*Carl Bodmer's 1835 painting above shows (at right center) the narrow entry
to Cave-in-Rock, a notorious den of thieves and killers on the Ohio River.*

were tempted by this promise of fun
and frolic were relieved of their cargoes and sometimes their lives. There
are differing accounts of who Wilson
was; one says that he was actually
Samuel Mason, a Revolutionary War
veteran who later went on to bigger
things down on the Natchez Trace.
Afterward, the cave was nothing but
a thieves' hangout, and its population
became so large and so evil that law
officers seldom made any attempt to
clean it out.

Farther down the Ohio, only a few
miles from where it empties into the
Mississippi, a river pirate named Colonel Fluger operated a quiet little business. Commonly called Old Plug, he

had a wife known as Pluggy, and two
or three helpers. His method of operation was to hail a flatboat some
distance upstream from his place, pretending usually to be a stranded traveler. As soon as he had been picked
up, he would secretly pick out some
calking between the planking on the
boat's bottom, timing it so that the
boat would get into trouble near his
place. His crew would put out in boats,
help the poor boatmen to rescue their
cargo, and then forget to save the boatmen. The Colonel's reward was almost
too good to be true: one time he
opened a bigger seam than he had in-
tended, the boat sank much faster than
he planned, and Old Plug went to a

place where he would scuttle no more.

Of all the blood-soaked wretches who ever afflicted the West, none ever equaled Micajah and Wiley Harpe, better known as Big and Little Harpe. They came over the mountains into eastern Tennessee sometime in the late 1790's with two women, one of whom was Big Harpe's wife; the other did not seem to belong to either. In Tennessee Wiley wooed and married a third woman. This strange household pretended to farm, but the brothers preferred to steal hogs and horses; they were caught, escaped, and then embarked on a career of brutal murder.

Their known victims in the next few weeks included a guest at a tavern near Knoxville, a peddler on the Wilderness Road, two travelers, and a young man who had joined them for protection in crossing a dangerous stretch of trail. The Harpes were captured again, es-caped again, and killed at least three more people; meanwhile, a soft-hearted jury of frontiersmen freed the three women who had been captured with the men.

The bloody troop went on toward the Ohio and put up at Cave-in-Rock for a time, but they were too much even for that depraved crew. One day a group of bandits, lounging in front of the cave, was startled by wild screams as a man and horse hurtled through the air from above and smashed almost into their midst. It turned out that the Harpe brothers, in a playful spirit, had tied a captive from a flatboat to a horse and then driven horse and rider from the bluff directly above the cave. Innocent fun or not, it was too much for the other hard-bitten characters of the cave, who sent the Harpes packing.

The strange and unholy crew, which now also included two very small chil-

The interior of Cave-in-Rock, once an Indian burial place.

The infamous robber John Murrell threatens one of his victims in this 1847 woodcut.

dren, moved south into Tennessee and then back into Kentucky. And in their wake the brothers left a trail of crime. Fortunately, one of their victims identified the Harpes, and a posse set out and caught up with them after a day's chase.

Little Harpe dashed into the woods and got away. Micajah took off down the trail, but he was fatally wounded by a lucky shot.

After his escape, Little Harpe wandered down to the Natchez Trace, where he joined up with Samuel Mason, the supposed proprietor of Wilson's Liquor Vault and House for Entertainment at Cave-in-Rock. Mason had tried river piracy for a while, but found it easier to let boatmen sell their own cargoes and then take their money from them while they were returning on the Trace.

The Trace should have satisfied Wiley Harpe's inclinations toward murder because there were plenty of travelers and no law, but when he heard there was a reward on Mason's

head, it gave him ideas. He and another man killed Mason and brought his head into Natchez. But Little Harpe was recognized; he and the other man were condemned and executed, and *their* heads were exhibited on stakes.

John A. Murrell stands near the top of the list of Mississippi Valley scoundrels, not because he was more bloodthirsty, but because he was smarter and had bigger ideas. Murrell came from Tennessee; he is said to have been tall, handsome, and strong. He might have made for himself an honorable career, but he went in the wrong direction (stories have it that his mother carefully taught him lessons in profitable wrongdoing), and progressed from small thieving to river piracy and highway robbery on the Natchez Trace.

Murrell saw that the steamboat and increasing settlement of the West would mean the end of the simple, pleasant days of piracy and highway robbery. He prepared for the change by traveling up and down the river, pretending to be a preacher—he could deliver quite an inspiring sermon—but actually organizing scoundrels into what he called a Mystic Brotherhood. There were secret handclasps and passwords and initiation ceremonies. His organization was said to have included several thousand men, among them some outwardly prominent and respectable persons. Its main business was stealing and selling slaves and horses, and it made a tremendous success of both, but Murrell had his eyes on bigger things: nothing less than a slave rebellion, the capture of New Orleans, Memphis, and Natchez, and the creation of an empire.

But one of his young recruits was a spy, and Murrell was arrested and brought to trial. However, all that could be proved against him was slave stealing, and for this he was sent to prison. Members of his clan tried to start a slave uprising to free their chief, but it was a failure. Murrell was eventually released from prison, and according to some accounts, was a peaceful blacksmith for a few years before he died of illness, still a comparatively young man.

Sometimes, to control the lawlessness that plagued the river towns, law-abiding citizens took matters into their own hands. That was what happened in Vicksburg.

Vicksburg's problem was gamblers, who infested the town in large numbers. Gambling was not against the law in those days, nor was it even considered in bad taste. Planters, businessmen, judges—all would gamble for entertainment and excitement. But it was not respectable to be a professional gambler, and in Vicksburg the professionals were becoming rude and insulting and were acting as though they owned the town. Moreover, there were so many of them—almost two hundred, it was said—that they felt safe in numbers.

Matters came to a head in the summer of 1835. One evening, a wealthy young planter went to one of the gambling houses. He was never seen again, and most of the townspeople were quick to believe that he had been murdered for his money. A few days later, a gentleman and lady walking through the streets were coarsely insulted. To top this off, the following day, the

Murrell, always a dashing criminal, wears his top hat as he rows with an accomplice across a rain-swept river, no doubt bent on some dark, secret mission.

This 1858 cartoon shows what the artist calls the usual "baggage" of river boat gamblers.

Fourth of July, a notorious gambler showed up at a public dinner and had to be thrown out. He returned with a pair of friends, and they created a commotion until they were thrown out again and the doors barred to them.

These events, coming in rapid succession, were too much for the good citizens of Vicksburg. They held a public meeting, and then served notice on the gamblers that anyone not able to show that he had a way of making an honest living must get out of town within twenty-four hours; ". . . all such persons found within the town limits after the expiration of this time shall receive thirty-nine lashes at the public whipping post."

It frightened away most of the gamblers. By steamboat and by horse, they streamed out of town with their women; however, a few of the most reckless remained, locked in one of the gambling houses. When a citizens' committee went to demand that they

leave, a gambler shot through the door, killing one of the committee. Now the furious citizens burst into the building and quickly subdued the rowdies.

What followed took little time. The prisoners—five of them—were taken to the town gallows, hanged without ceremony, and buried at the foot of the gallows. A group of citizens went down to Natchez, asking that similar steps be taken with the community under the bluff. The rabble there did not wait for steamboats but loaded themselves on flatboats and every other available craft and shoved out into the river. Most of them undoubtedly ended up in New Orleans, which was always more hospitable to undesirables.

The popular image of the river boat gambler is of an elegantly dressed man, smiling and friendly but hard-eyed, striking up a friendly poker game on one of the luxury steamboats. There were, of course, professional gamblers who rode the packets, but if there was anything they wanted to avoid, it was to look like professional gamblers. They pretended to be cattle buyers, farmers, lightning rod salesmen, anything but what they were. Often they worked in pairs; if so, they tried to come aboard at different landings, and would not talk to each other until introduced by a third party.

The modern photograph at right of one of the remaining stretches of the historic Natchez Trace indicates what a perfect setting for ambush this shadowy trail was in the days of Murrell and other thieves and murderers.

COLLECTION OF RUTH FERRIS

Shown above is the crucial moment when a river boat gambler gets one of the passengers to put up his money. The devices at right were used in gambling games—the cup (top) for chuck-a-luck and the "goose" (below) for keno.

Some gamblers claimed to be honest, and it is just possible they were. But most were card sharps who used every trick from marked cards to dealing from the bottom of the deck. The crooked gambler's strategy was usually the same: to find a man with money, to get involved in a friendly game with him, to let him win for a while until he was feeling confident, and then to move in for the kill by dealing the victim a hand so good that he would bid recklessly, while giving himself (or his partner) a hand just a little bit better.

A gambler had to think fast and move fast at times. One of them, after parting a group of men from their money and other valuables, overheard his victims plotting to kill him so as to recover their losses. He hid, but sent word to the pilot to swing close to shore at the first chance, so he could leap to safety. But when the moment came, he landed in river mud where he stuck up to his waist. His victims immediately discovered him and started shooting, but fortunately for the helplessly stuck gambler, their aim was poor, and the boat rapidly drew out of range. Slaves in a nearby field heard his calls and pulled him out of the mud with a pole.

Another time the same gambler was in exactly the same predicament: he was hiding on a boat from a gang of toughs whose money he had won and who had later got drunk and set out for revenge. This time he changed into filthy clothing, blackened his face, and went down among the roustabouts where he went unnoticed until the next stop. Then he picked up a piece of freight, carried it down the gangplank in the line of roustabouts, and kept right on going while his enemies were still seeking him among the well-dressed passengers.

But sometimes the gambler was caught. Once, on the *Eclipse,* a card sharp won $1,000 from a young man in a way that other passengers thought just might be cheating. They held a trial and sentenced the gambler either to return the money or to spend an hour tied to the connecting rod of the engine. The gambler chose the latter punishment. The connecting rod connected the piston of the engine to the crankshaft of the paddle wheel; as the piston moved back and forth, ten feet to a stroke, so did the connecting rod, turning the crank that churned the paddle wheel.

A rope was tied to the rod while the other end of it was looped around the gambler's neck, and he started his dangerous back-and-forth walk as the steamboat got under way. His path was narrow and ten feet long; he had to walk at just the right speed and turn at just the right moment as the connecting rod changed its direction. If his judgment had gone wrong even for a moment, his neck would have been snapped. Once he was asked if he was ready to return the money. "Go away, I have no time to talk," he said. When his hour was up, he was released, but no one had anything to do with him for the rest of the trip.

Many a gambler had to make a quick exit from a boat on which he had been accused of cheating. In this illustration—taken from the memoirs of a retired Mississippi gambler published in the 1880's—a fleeing card sharp wades ashore while one of his victims gets in a parting shot.

9. Races and Wrecks

Working furiously in the dead of night, the roustabouts in this 1867 print are wooding up their steamboat as rapidly as possible to prevent it from falling behind schedule.

People on the river were more interested in a steamboat's speed than in anything else about her. Careful records were kept of the time between various important cities—New Orleans to Natchez, Louisville to St. Louis, St. Louis to St. Paul—and a boat that had made the fastest time for one of these runs was said to "hold the horns." A pair of gilded deer horns, usually mounted on the pilothouse, was the boat's boast to the world of her speed, and as soon as another boat made a faster trip, the horns were handed over to the new champion. But it was more than pride that made a captain want to take the horns: a fast boat attracted more passengers and freight.

Where men were so interested in speed, the natural result was steamboat racing. It was thrilling—and it was dangerous. Newspaper editors could attack it, legislatures could pass laws against it, insurance companies could raise their rates because of it, but nothing stopped it. When two evenly matched boats found themselves in the same stretch of river, it just seemed natural that the black smoke should come pouring from the stacks, the paddle wheels turn a little faster, and the passengers rush to the rails and cheer and shout.

Not all races were unplanned, chance encounters on the river. Sometimes a race between two well-known boats would be announced weeks in advance. The vessels would be carefully prepared. Anything that added extra weight would be removed. En-

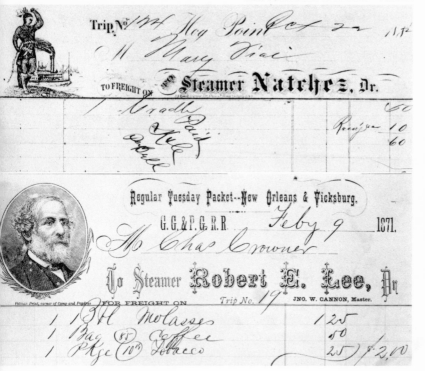

The freight bills above, issued by the Natchez *(top) and its rival the* Robert E. Lee, *carried elegantly printed letterheads. Captain John W. Cannon, wily skipper of the* Robert E. Lee *and victor in the great race with the* Natchez, *is shown at the right.*

gines and boilers would be put in their best operating condition. No way-freight for smaller towns would be taken because the boats would stop only at larger ports, and then only touch-and-go. Few passengers were carried; they were a nuisance because they always ran to the side of the boat where something was happening, making the boat list and not run at its best. Fuel would be arranged for beforehand, waiting in barges that the boat could hitch onto and tow along-side while frantically working roust-abouts transferred the fuel. And a good supply of pitch, turpentine, fat

sides of bacon, or anything else that would produce a roaring fire would be stored aboard.

There were many notable races, but the most famous of all was the one between the *Robert E. Lee* and the *Natchez* in 1870. This was the sixth *Natchez* built by Captain Tom Leathers, and he is said to have designed it especially to beat the *Lee*. For many months the two fast vessels had been operating between New Orleans and St. Louis but on different days. Then Captain Leathers threw down a challenge, saying that he would leave New Orleans at the same time as the *Lee*.

As the day neared, excitement grew greater and greater. Each boat had its loud and loyal champions, who not only argued but bet heavily. The telegraph kept the rest of the country informed, and even carried the news to Europe on the Atlantic cable. In the meantime the boats were made ready. Captain Leathers was confident of the *Natchez* and made no unusual preparations. But Captain John W. Cannon of the *Lee* prepared his boat as if readying a warship for battle.

All the glass in the *Lee's* pilothouse was removed, as were the steam escape pipes, and various doors, windows, shutters, and projections—anything that would cause air resistance. Hoists, anchors, rigging, and anything else not absolutely necessary during the race was taken off. When Captain Cannon was finished, the *Robert E. Lee* was an odd-looking steamboat.

When the time came to leave New Orleans, the *Lee* was tied up by a single line, with a man standing by with an axe. At exactly five o'clock in the afternoon, a single tap was given on the *Lee's* bell, the axe flashed through the line, and the boat was on its way. The maneuver gave Captain Cannon a start of three or four minutes, and the *Natchez* never made it up. Above Vicksburg, *Natchez* supporters received a shock. Here a steamboat, the *Frank Pargoud,* waited with steam up and loaded with fuel; she raced alongside the *Lee,* and the two were tied together and ran at reduced speed while fuel was loaded onto the *Lee.*

In spite of this, the *Natchez* more than held her own and was still very much in the race when the boats ran into heavy fog above the mouth of the Ohio. Captain Cannon, with four pilots aboard, kept pushing the *Robert E. Lee* into the fog, slowly perhaps, but always moving. Sometimes the boat veered away from disaster at the last moment, but luck was with the *Lee.* As for Captain Leathers, he decided to tie up until the fog cleared.

The *Robert E. Lee* steamed past the finish point at St. Louis at 11:25 A.M. on July 4, 1870, while thousands on the levee cheered. It had taken her three days, eighteen hours, and fourteen minutes to make the trip. The *Natchez* did not arrive until some six and a half hours later.

Supporters of the *Natchez* made a loud protest, complaining that the use of another steamboat for fueling, as well as other actions of Captain Cannon, violated all rules. Bets in some places were canceled as a result of the dispute. And that was just about the end of racing on the Mississippi. In making such a professional thing of it, Captain Cannon had taken the fun away. Besides, the golden days of steamboating began to wane soon after as railroads spread into the West. Before long no one cared about building a faster steamboat to take the horns from the *Robert E. Lee.*

There were more than enough dangers in steamboating at any time, but the quest for speed made matters worse than they need have been. A

This exciting painting, done after the famous race between the Robert E. Lee *and the* Natchez *in 1870, pictures the two boats, their smokestacks spouting flames, racing upriver on a moonlit night. Although the steamboats are shown accurately enough, they were never "neck and neck" as the scene indicates; the* Robert E. Lee *was ahead of the* Natchez *consistently from the time it left New Orleans until its victorious arrival in St. Louis.*

captain trying to set a new record or show his heels to another boat would cram the fireboxes with fuel, throw in pitch or oil or fat sides of pork to make the fire burn faster and hotter, tie down the safety valves to raise the steam pressure to a screaming pitch—and hope for the best. A little sanity prevailed toward the end, with government inspection of boilers and sealing of safety valves to make it harder to tamper with them (the *Lee* and the *Natchez* almost certainly stayed within their safe pressures), but it is a wonder that most races did not end with both vessels exploding or burning.

The greatest danger was fire. Michael Chevalier, a Frenchman who traveled in the West, was amazed at the carelessness he saw. "The Americans show a singular indifference in regard to fires," he wrote. "They smoke without the least concern in the midst of half-open cotton-bales, with which a boat is loaded; they ship gunpowder with no more precaution than if it were so much maize or salt pork, and leave objects packed in straw right in the torrent of sparks that issue from the chimneys." Chevalier added that the important thing seemed to be not the safety of people but to have steamboats moving as fast as possible and at the least expense.

If danger from fire existed even during ordinary travel, it was much worse during a race with the fireboxes overheated and the chimneys pouring out sparks. And since the steamboats were so flimsily constructed, once a fire started there was seldom any stopping it. In 1832, the *Brandywine* and the *Hudson* were above Memphis, racing. The *Brandywine* was behind but catching up as her engine-room crew fed a roaring fire with resin; then sparks fell on some crates of carriage wheels wrapped in straw, and in minutes the entire boat was ablaze. The pilot ran her for shore but grounded on a bar a quarter of a mile short of it; the crew put over the boat's yawl but immediately swamped it. More than one hundred lost their lives that day, victims of steamboat racing.

In 1837, the *Ben Sherrod* was trailing in a race with the *Prairie* about twenty miles below Natchez when her overheated fireboxes set fire to fuel wood piled next to them. The pilot headed the boat for shore, but the ropes running from steering wheel to rudder burned through, and he could not steer. The fire set off a number of barrels of whiskey which exploded, spraying the flaming liquid over everything. Then the boilers let go with a roar, and finally fire reached forty barrels of gunpowder which ripped the already shattered boat to bits. Half an hour later, the *Columbus* arrived and was taking people out of the water when another boat, the *Alton,* came up and steamed over many of the survivors, drowning them. That race cost at least 150 lives. As for the *Prairie,* the other boat in the race, her captain saw the *Sherrod* go up in flames but did not bother to turn back. He simply reported the tragedy at his next stop.

Tales of the Mississippi

On April 25, 1838, the steamer Moselle *(above), her boilers under severe strain, exploded on the Ohio a mile below Cincinnati and eighty-one people were killed.*

The big side-wheelers United States *and* America *(right) collided on the Ohio near Warsaw, Kentucky, in 1868. Both boats caught fire, causing a heavy loss of life.*

These melancholy events happened time and time again, and many of them were due to near-idiocy on the part of those handling the boats. The *Moselle*, in 1838, was not only the finest on the Ohio, but according to her owner, Captain Perrin, the fastest in America. On this trip he was out to beat the time of a rival to St. Louis; he had stopped briefly at Cincinnati to take aboard some emigrants, but even during the stop the fires were being fed furiously to build very high pressure in the boilers, whose safety valves were tied down. One passenger looked in the engine room, saw the steam gauge, and quickly left the boat. Just as the *Moselle* was going out into the river again, all four of her boilers blew up. Fragments of timbers and boilers and human bodies fell as far as the Kentucky shore, a quarter of a mile away. There were eighty-one known dead, fifty-five missing.

But speed did not cause all the accidents. Steamboats caught fire, had boiler explosions, hit snags, collided, and in the upper river, occasionally wrecked themselves on floating ice, when racing was the last thing on the captain's mind. In 1856, *Lloyd's Steamboat Directory* listed eighty-seven "major disasters" that had occurred on western rivers up to that time; in many of these, more than one hundred lives had been lost. There were also listed 220 "minor disasters," in most of which people were killed, sometimes forty or fifty. Between 1811 and 1850, more than 4,000 people were

The Belle Creole, *shown here at her New Orleans berth, had a short, accident-ridden career. Launched in 1845, she sank in 1846 but was raised and put back into commission; she exploded in 1849 and was repaired again. She was finally retired from service in 1851.*

killed or injured in steamboat accidents on the Mississippi.

Boilers exploded many times when it seemed as though no strain was being put on them. On a November afternoon in 1849, the *Louisiana* was just backing away from the New Orleans levee when her boilers burst. Pieces flew everywhere, causing death and destruction. One jagged piece of boiler metal whirled through the air, cut a mule in two, bounced some distance, and killed a drayman and his horse. People on shore were killed and injured as far as two hundred feet away. Some of those on the *Louisiana* were blown high in the air—witnesses estimated as high as two hundred feet. On one side of the *Louisiana* at the levee, the *Storm* was tied up; she had just arrived from Cincinnati, and her passengers were still aboard. The terrific force of the blast wrecked her upper works, blew her fifty yards from the levee, and killed fifteen people on board. The shattered *Louisiana* sank within ten minutes.

Many steamboats were lost on snags. The *Shepherdess* came to such an unhappy end only three miles above St. Louis, on the bitterly cold night of January 3, 1844. Within five minutes the hull, the engines, and the boilers were under water, and water was entering the cabins. Captain Howell, who had just bought the *Shepherdess* and was making his first trip with her, helped rouse the sleeping passengers and get them up onto the hurricane deck. The yawl was launched, but there were no oars in it, and it had to be paddled ashore with a broom.

As the *Shepherdess* drifted, she struck another snag which threw her almost on her side, hurling a number of people into the icy river. The shock tore loose engines, boilers, and chimneys, and Captain Howell was dragged overboard by the wreckage and drowned. Then the stricken craft drifted into a bank where more passengers were knocked into the river. Here the upper works tore loose from the hull. A steamboat tied up nearby without fire in its boilers, put out its yawl, and rescued many people, and by three in the morning a ferryboat came up from St. Louis and rescued the last of the half-frozen survivors from the cabin. Between forty and seventy were lost; in those haphazard days, it was seldom known just how many were aboard, or how many of those were lost.

Hundreds of steamboats came to violent ends in the Mississippi and its tributaries, but the worst tragedy of all was the loss of the steamboat *Sultana*. It was almost the end of April, 1865; the Civil War was just over when the big side-wheeler *Sultana* pulled into Vicksburg to take aboard soldiers and officers, most of them just released from Southern prison camps, for return to the North. The boat was meant to carry fewer than four hundred passengers; now, as she steamed upriver, an estimated 2,500 were crammed aboard her. The *Sultana* was having other troubles, too; her boilers were in bad condition, but her engineers had been told to patch things up as best they could and keep her running.

While passing a group of islands called Paddy's Hen and Chickens above Memphis, about two in the morning of April 27, the *Sultana's* tired boilers exploded. Then the wreck caught fire. Those who survived the explosion had no choice other than to jump into the water, and many either did not know how to swim or were so weak from their imprisonment that they could not stay afloat. The water was high, the current strong, and rescuing steamboats did not show up until dawn. The count of dead was indefinite as it always was in those easygoing days, but the best-informed estimates are that about 1,500 died.

Once in a very great while an accident could be more comic than tragic.

The *Belle Air* was coming down the upper Mississippi in floodtime in the spring of 1844, and like many boats when the river was over its banks, had taken a short cut across country. But the pilot found himself in strange territory, taking the boat right down the main street of Chester, Illinois. The boat bumped into a three-story building and knocked the top story into the water, then changed course and smashed a stone mill. Next she bounced off several brick buildings, wrecked the county jail, and finally blundered her way out into the open again.

The *Belle Air* came through almost undamaged. She continued her trip without further incident down to New Orleans. There, a few minutes away from a mooring, she clumsily ran into a ferryboat, and in a sinking condition, just managed to reach the levee.

This rare photograph of the Sultana, *her decks jammed with Union soldiers heading up the Mississippi at the end of the Civil War, was taken just a day or two before her boilers exploded near Memphis, killing about 1,500 men.*

10. Tall Tales and Legends

Rivermen seemed to possess a talent for having a good time. Whether they listened to tunes played on a fiddle, like the raftsmen in this 1844 painting by the American artist William Baldwin, or spun tall tales, they enjoyed life.

Long before the white man saw the Mississippi River, the Indians already had their own legends about it. When the French explorers Marquette and Joliet started down the Mississippi in canoes, they were warned that there was a demon living in the river whose roar could be heard for great distances, and who would drag them down into the depths where he lived.

Many years later, Negro roustabouts on the lower river were certain that a frightening creature lived in their part of the Mississippi, and they knew much more about him than the Indians did about the river demon in the north. His name was Old Al and he was a giant alligator who wore a gold crown and smoked a pipe. He was huge beyond imagining; he pushed up sand bars for steamboats to go aground on, he swished his tail to make currents, and sometimes he picked a roustabout off a steamboat for lunch. Sometimes a weary roustabout would drop a pinch of tobacco overboard, a gift for Al's pipe. For when the alligator king smoked, it created a heavy fog so that the steamboat had to tie up, and then there would be a rest from handling heavy bales of cotton.

There were plenty of superstitions about the river, especially among the people at its lower end. Washing one's face in the river was said to bring good luck. Louisiana Negroes believed it bad luck to throw an animal or fowl into the river. And there was widespread belief that the Mississippi never gave up a body—although it is hard to know how such an idea could persist when many river dwellers must have seen it proved false.

Steamboatmen had their special superstitions. There is something about working afloat—from a salt-water ship to a ferryboat—that makes a man extra careful about unknown forces around him, and rivermen were no exception. Sometimes, of course, they were just having fun, as when they said that an old steamboatman turned into a white mule when he died. But when they claimed that it was bad luck to have a preacher and a gray mare aboard at the same time, they were in dead earnest. In *Life on the Mississippi*, Mark Twain writes jokingly about this belief, but it was not a joking matter to most boatmen:

". . . The Grand Chain . . . is a chain of sunken rocks admirably arranged to capture and kill steamboats on bad nights. A good many steamboat corpses lie buried there, out of sight; among the rest my first friend the *Paul Jones;* she knocked her bottom out, and went down like a pot, so the historian told me—Uncle Mumford. He said she had a gray mare aboard, and a preacher. To me, this sufficiently accounted for the disaster; as it did, of course, to Mumford, who added:

" 'But there are many ignorant people who would scoff at such a matter, and call it superstition. But you will always notice that they are people who have never travelled with a gray mare and a preacher. I went down the river once in such a company. We grounded at Bloody Island; we grounded at Hanging Dog; we grounded just below this same Commerce; we jolted Beaver Dam Rock; we hit one of the worst breaks in the 'Graveyard' behind Goose Island; we had a roustabout killed in a fight; we burst a boiler; broke a shaft; collapsed a flue; and went into Cairo with nine feet of water in the hold—may have been more, may have been less. I remember it as if it were yesterday. The men lost their heads with terror. They painted the mare blue, in sight of town, and threw the preacher overboard, or we should not have arrived at all. The preacher was fished out and saved. He acknowledged, himself, that he had been to blame.'"

The Mississippi inspired all sorts of tall tales. There were giant steamboats like the *Hurronico* (her hull was jointed so she could get around the

On quiet stretches of the river, pilothouse regulars filled the air with river lore and swapped their highly-colored recollections.

bends); the *E. Jenkins* (it took from spring until fall for her huge wheel to make one turn, her lowest-paid roustabouts got chicken and watermelon every meal, and her pilot refused to work unless he had champagne for breakfast); and the *Jim Johnson* (her smokestacks were so tall that after the fires were put out in the fall, smoke was still coming out in the spring).

If men worked a bit hard to make up such tales, that was not the case when rivermen got to talking about the muddiness of the river; then they were talking right from the heart. In *Life on the Mississippi*, Mark Twain, on his return visit to the river, meets a young man new to the region who is puzzled about what to do when thirsty —he could drink the Mississippi River water only if he had "some other water to wash it with." And Twain goes on:

"Here was a thing which had not changed; a score of years had not affected this water's mulatto complexion in the least; a score of centuries would succeed no better, perhaps. It comes out of the turbulent, bank-caving Missouri, and every tumblerful of it holds nearly an acre of land in solution. I got this fact from the bishop of the diocese. If you will let your glass stand half an hour, you can separate the land from the water as easy as Genesis; and then you will find them both good: the one good to eat, the other good to drink. The land is very nourishing, the water is thoroughly wholesome. The one appeases hunger; the other, thirst. But the natives do not take them separately, but together, as nature mixed them. When they find an inch of mud in the bottom of a glass, they stir it up, and then take the draught as they would gruel. It is difficult for a stranger to get used to this batter, but once used to it he will prefer it to water. This is really the case. It is good for steamboating, and good to drink; but it is worthless for all other purposes, except baptizing."

As Twain said, the muddiness of the Mississippi comes from the Missouri. And that, as all rivermen insist, is *really* a muddy stream. It is, they say, the only river where the dust blows out of the river bed in great clouds and the catfish must come up to the surface to sneeze. It is so thick with dissolved farms that sometimes it cracks as it goes around a bend, and in dry seasons Missouri water is drunk with a fork. Even in its ordinary state, Missouri water must be stirred before it can be poured from one container to another. A man jumping into the Missouri is more apt to break a leg than drown.

The upper Mississippi became dusty one year, too, but because of low water rather than silt in the water. That was during the Civil War when one pilot complained that the channel was so dry that his paddle wheels kicked up dust. Another said that his boat could run without trouble in the moisture on the outside of a pitcher of ice water but that he was having a great deal of trouble in the river below St. Paul. And there was talk of giving up steamboating on the upper Mississippi and lay-ing a railroad track right up the bed of the river—but the plan was dropped because it was feared there would not be enough water to supply the boilers of locomotives on the line.

A completely different kind of story of the river is the account of the *Drennan Whyte* and the treasure she carried. How much of that story is true and how much is legend there is no way of knowing. The *Whyte*, so the story goes, was carrying one hundred thousand dollars in gold on an upriver trip in the autumn of 1850 when she blew up and sank in deep water a few miles above Natchez.

The owners of the boat attempted to salvage the gold, but the river was not ready to give it up, and the salvage vessel caught fire and sank, killing sixteen men. It was a year before another attempt could be made, and this time the salvage boat, unable to locate the wreck, ran aground and was almost sunk. Salvage attempts were given up, and the *Whyte* was left to the river.

Twenty years passed, and a down-on-his-luck farmer was digging a well for his cattle on land near the river-bank on his farm in Mississippi. His name was Ancil Fortune, and by odd coincidence he was the son of the man who had been captain of the boat that had made the second unsuccessful at-tempt to salvage the gold from the *Drennan Whyte*. He had heard the story of the *Whyte* from his father many times, and now, as he scraped away at a metal object he had struck and uncovered enough to show it to

Life along the Mississippi has always fascinated authors. This striking poster announced the 1914 publication of a novel about the river by the distinguished Southern writer George Washington Cable.

be the smokestack of a steamboat, the thought came to him that it might—just might—be the lost boat. True, this was much farther downstream than the *Drennan Whyte* had sunk, but his father had been unable to locate the wreck although he had grappled the river bottom for miles. It was possible that the powerful currents of the spring floods had dragged the wreck a long distance.

However, his legal right to the land was clouded, and if he started digging and word got around that he was after the treasure of the *Drennan Whyte,* people would chase him out in a hurry. So he filled the well again, quietly planted willows over the entire area, and then waited patiently for five years while a thicket of trees grew up.

Only then did he start digging, protected in the middle of the small grove from any observers. It was a giant's task for a man who still had the full-time job of running a farm and feeding a family. For a long time he did not even know whether he was on a wild goose chase, but one day he turned up a brass plate with the name "Drennan Whyte" on it, and that doubt was removed.

There was an enormous amount of earth to be moved. Every cabin had been packed solid with silt, and each had to be explored. There were cave-ins, and twice the hole filled with water and had to be emptied with a bucket. At last, one spring day in 1881, almost thirty-one years after the *Drennan Whyte* had sunk, and eleven years after Ancil Fortune's shovel had struck the top of the steamboat's rusty smoke-stack, he uncovered an iron chest and broke it open to find that at last the treasure was his.

He was a poor man no more. For a while he gloated over the box of gold coins, and then he started across the field for home to get a sack to start removing the gold in. On the way he caught his foot in a root, twisted his leg, and falling heavily, snapped the bone. His family found him and brought him home.

That night it rained—a long downpour that lasted for many days and extended far up the river valley above. The river rose, banks caved, and the current, which for years had been gradually swinging away from where the *Drennan Whyte* lay and building up dry land between, now moved back. When Ancil Fortune was able to drag himself to the window many days later, the grove of willows was gone, and the river once again ran deep and swift over the spot where the *Whyte* had lain so long.

Then, so the story goes, Fortune managed to half-hop, half-drag himself across the field and straight into the river to die. And there, perhaps, he found the treasure once again, to stay with it forever.

Sometimes a story of the river has an aura of the supernatural about it. Long ago, on a stretch of the river between Natchez, Mississippi, and Baton Rouge, Louisiana, there was one of those great sweeping horseshoe curves so common on the river; this one was known as Raccourci Bend. During one wild night of thunder and lightning in 1825, the river broke across the narrow base of the horseshoe and within a few hours a new channel was established.

An unfortunate steamboat was coming downstream shortly after the river began to break through. The pilot had no idea a cutoff was being formed, and since nothing could be seen in the dark and rain, he quite naturally followed the old channel. The water was already falling there; the boat scraped across a new bar, shaved another, and only a timely flash of lightning enabled the bewildered pilot to bear away from a snag where the channel should have been clear.

Nothing was as it should have been, and finally the pilot began to curse, swearing a mighty oath that he would find his way out in spite of anything that all the powers of heaven and hell might do to try to stop him. It proved a very unwise thing to say, because he is still said to be trying to get his steamboat out of that now-forgotten channel.

Over the years, Raccourci Bend became no more than a series of stagnant swamps, and only old-timers remembered when it had been part of the river. But many times since that night, steamboatmen have told of looking down the abandoned channel as their boats passed at night and of seeing the phantom steamer of Raccourci Bend. It seemed to happen most often on a dismal, rainy night (the sort when a man might have several drinks of whiskey to keep the chill out). There, shining with a faint, blue light like a will-o'-the-wisp, the steamboat would be seen completely lost in the once-familiar channel. Sometimes the sound of her bell could be heard, and the splash of her paddle wheels, and occasionally even the far-off voice of the pilot, still cursing the fates that had done such strange things to Raccourci Bend.

The average life span of the western steamboat was short. The eerie, moldering hulks of wrecked vessels abandoned on the riverbanks, like the one in this 1888 drawing, gave rise to many a ghostly tale or legend.

Harper's Weekly, 1888

11. New Times on the River

The Civil War brought havoc and hard times to the Mississippi, as shown graphically in this Currier and Ives print. Many of the graceful packets were sunk by gunboats, or burned to prevent their capture.

135

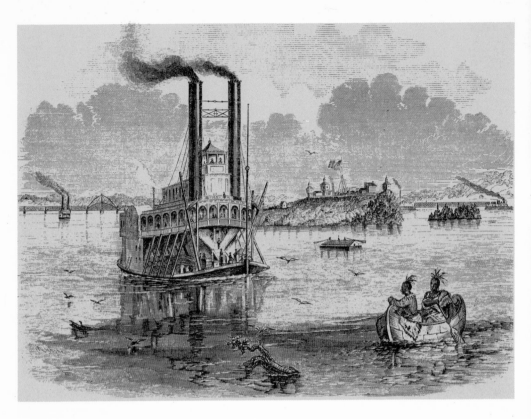

The Rock Island Railroad Bridge, so despised by the big steamboat interests, is visible in the background of this woodcut of 1858.

The Civil War split the Mississippi in two—one part controlled by the Union, the other by the Confederacy —and the exciting, bustling, busy days came to an end. Steamboats traveled the western rivers on grim errands now, hauling troops, carrying supplies and ammunition, transporting wounded. Beautiful boats were sunk by enemy guns, or were destroyed to keep them from falling into hostile hands. Many others were tied up and rotted at their wharves.

Strange new craft appeared—squat, deadly ironclad gunboats that dueled with each other and with guns on shore, and many brave men died for control of the Mississippi and a number of its branches. But that is a story of its own, too big to tell here. The end

of the war found the river in sad condition. Many of its steamboats were gone, plantations were ruined, and most of the levee system built for flood protection on the lower river had been ruined during the years of neglect.

By 1866 the steamboat boom had resumed, as if it had never been interrupted. New packets began coming out of the boat yards again, some of the biggest, handsomest, fastest boats the river had ever seen. This period, in the late 1860's and 1870's, was the time of such beautiful, swift boats as the *Robert E. Lee* and the *Natchez*, the *Great Republic*, and the third *J. M. White*.

Then the packets began to grow fewer and fewer. A rival had "taken the horns" from the steamboats, a rival that had a lot more freedom in choosing where it would go.

The railroads had first appeared in the West in the late 1840's; by 1854 they were not only threading their way over much of the territory east of the Mississippi, but one line, the Rock Island, reached the river at Rock Island, Illinois, and pushed a bridge across. River people were alarmed by the rapid spread of the iron rails. Steamboatmen foresaw the loss of business, while the citizens of river towns like St. Louis were afraid a shift of commerce from river to railroads would mean the loss of their trade advantages. They had tried to have construction of the Rock Island bridge stopped on the legal ground that it interfered with free passage of the river, but that had failed. Now they waited for an accident so that they could go to court.

The accident came in May of 1856. The *Effie Afton*, a popular boat of the day, had just backed out from the landing above the bridge and was straightened out in the current when something went wrong. She hit one of the piers of the bridge, swung into the other, stuck there, and caught fire. She was destroyed and so was part of the bridge.

Stern-wheel towboats like the Iron Age, *seen here with stacks hinged to clear a bridge, continued to work the rivers despite railroads.*

COLLECTION OF A. S. HINCHEY

On July 4, 1874, St. Louis celebrated the opening of the Eads Bridge, a railroad span more than a mile long that was one of the engineering marvels of the day.

The old photograph above, taken near Rosedale, Mississippi, shows a big steam crane covering the banks of the unruly Mississippi with asphalt to restrict the ravages of flood erosion.

Attempts were also made to tame the Ohio. The crowd on the riverbank in the photograph at right has gathered to watch the opening of the Ohio's first navigation dam in October, 1885.

The owners of the *Effie Afton* at once sued the railroad. They claimed, first, that the river was the great waterway of the valley and could not legally be obstructed by any bridge, and second, that this particular bridge was placed in an especially bad way so as to be a menace to navigation. Because the case was so important, both sides hired crews of talented lawyers; on the side of the Rock Island Railroad was an attorney named Abraham Lincoln.

Lincoln handled much of the argument for his side. Against the claim of the river people that no one had a right to build a bridge across the Mississippi, he took the position that "one man has as good a right to cross a river as another has to sail up or down it." He asked whether the products of the fertile lands west of the Mississippi must for all time be unloaded from trains to ferries and then back on trains to get them to the East.

As for this bridge being badly placed, Lincoln discussed the currents around its piers and showed he knew more about them than did the pilot of the *Effie Afton,* whose job it was to be acquainted with such things. He suggested that if the boat had been ably handled it would not have gotten into trouble. In the end, the jury could not agree, and the whole issue dragged on for several years in Washington until it was finally settled in favor of the

right of the railroads to bridge the Mississippi.

Very soon the railroads were crossing at other points, and laying tracks along the river so that river towns also became railroad towns. It took a while before the railroad lines became widespread enough to be a serious rival to the river boats, but within ten years or so after the Civil War, river traffic was beginning to suffer. The packets made their last stands along stretches of

141

river where the railroads had not yet reached; their mellow whistles echoed finally only along the upper Missouri in the Dakotas and Montana. Then the rails of the Great Northern and the Northern Pacific railroads were laid across the plains, and there, too, the whistle of the locomotive took the place of that of the steamboat.

The river now became a work-horse river. The white pine forests of Minne- sota and Wisconsin continued to send down huge rafts of saw logs and lum- ber, each guided by its stern-wheel towboat, until well into the present century. Then the lumberjacks finally cut their way through the forests that had once seemed inexhaustible; they took their axes and saws and headed out toward the Pacific, leaving the cookhouse and the bunkhouse in the woods to rot. On the upper Mississippi

the stern-wheel rafters were tied up and also left to rot.

But there were other heavy cargoes besides logs: coal, steel, building stone, gravel, oil; where there was something big and heavy to be moved and no hurry about it, no railroad could possibly do the job so cheaply as a husky towboat pushing several barges tied together with steel cable. The towboats themselves remained un-

changed for a long time; it has been only in very recent years that churning screw propellers have taken the place of the big, splashing stern paddle wheels, and even today it is not too difficult to find an old stern-wheeler still hard at work.

When Mark Twain returned to the river in 1882, he was struck by the way the government had marked the channel with lights—in fact, as a pilot who had learned to navigate at night by nothing more than starlight, he had a feeling the government was over-doing it a bit, and was marking crossings so plainly that a steamboat "can take herself through them without any help, after she has been through once." Twain was also impressed by the way the government kept the river free of snags, and by the electric searchlight which took the dangers out of a close place on a dark night. But he did not wholly approve because these things "knocked the romance out of piloting, to a large extent."

What would he think of the river today—the upper Mississippi, at least—on learning that it has been turned into what amounts to a canal? Twenty-seven dams have backed the water into a series of pools to keep an even depth of water for navigation, with locks to lift towboats and barges up and down. The Ohio has long been similarly pro-

JACK ZEHRT, FPG

The River Queen, *one of the last of the Mississippi packets, is unceremoniously delivered to her final resting place, lashed to a diesel towboat's barge tow. The* River Queen *is now used as a river museum in Hannibal.*

vided with dams and locks, and the same arrangement lets husky diesel towboats push their barges of coal up the Monongahela where the first western steamboats were built. Even the wild Missouri is now being tamed by dams, with towboats and barges moving peacefully where pilots once kept a wary eye out for hostile Indians.

River traffic is far from dead, but it is not the kind that supports most of the smaller towns on its banks. A tow of barges of crude oil almost a quarter of a mile long does not stop at many landings. So the landing levee has crumbled away, the old boat yard has become overgrown with willows, and the town which had looked to the river now has turned the other way. Some towns have made the change very well; others faded away when the packet boats tied up for the last time.

Read's Landing is only one of many examples. On a good map, it is possible to find Read's Landing, Minne-

sota, at the lower end of the wide place in the Mississippi called Lake Pepin. But it will have to be a good map, because Read's is not a very big place any more. Yet there was a day when Read's Landing was one of the greatest wheat shipping ports of the country, and in the 1850's it had seventeen hotels to take care of the river boat travelers who stopped there. A good many other sleepy river towns could tell similar stories of past glory.

There was a day when rivermen said that a leash would never be put on the Mississippi—and certainly it is not completely tamed now—but today a great deal of the wildness has been taken out of it. The river is not even free to change its channel the way it was in the old days. Whenever an important stretch of bank is threatened now, the Army Engineers Corps, which has charge of this work, moves in and goes to work.

The engineers no longer trust the river even to make its own cutoffs, but

do it themselves by cutting across the necks of horseshoe curves. In one period in recent years, between 1933 and 1942, they made fifteen such cuts and shortened the river by 142 miles. Thus, it seems unlikely that some stormy night a towboat with barges will be caught when the river makes a cutoff, creating a legend about the phantom towboat of such-and-such bend.

The engineers have been battling this giant antagonist for a long time now, and they had a lot to learn. They drove pilings to save the banks—but the river brushed them aside. They shaved back threatened banks and paved them with rock and built wing dams to deflect the current, but when the river made up its mind it wanted to get through, it usually elbowed rocks

This great sea of people assembled at the Pittsburgh docks on October 31, 1911, to celebrate the hundredth anniversary of steam navigation on western rivers. This dramatic picture was taken from a telephone pole.

and wing dams aside and went where it wanted. Then the engineers found that great, thick mats woven of willows resisted quite well the pounding of the current. Today they are using vast mattresses made of concrete slabs tied together with stainless steel cables. These are unrolled from barges to tie down the bank where the river is eating it away (with such means, perhaps even Napoleon, Arkansas, could have been saved).

All this work to tie down the river should not discourage those who like to think of it as a free-flowing, unconquered stream. It is just as well that it is no longer permitted to run completely wild, dealing death and destruction in times of high water, as it did for so long. But at the same time it is impossible to imagine the Mississippi as a tame, gentle stream. No matter what they do to confine it, the massive, muddy body of water that rolls endlessly out of the north to the Gulf will always be the Great River.

GJON MILI

The Mississippi, *a proud old stern-wheeler launched in 1882, is shown here in 1955 still working the river, her days of glory long past. At the time this photograph was taken she was being used by the United States Army engineers to haul supplies for levee-building operations.*

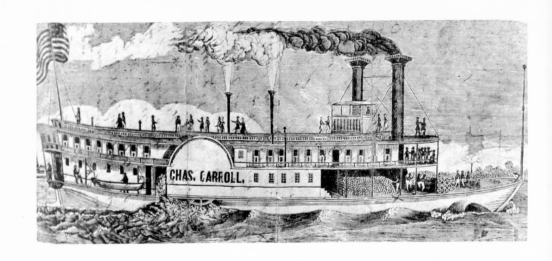

AMERICAN HERITAGE PUBLISHING CO., INC.

BOOK DIVISION

Editor
Richard M. Ketchum

———— * ————

JUNIOR LIBRARY

Managing Editor
Stephen W. Sears

Art Director
Emma Landau

Assistant Editors
John Ratti
Mary Lee Settle

Picture Researchers
CHIEF: Julia B. Potts
Dennis A. Dinan
Mary Leverty

Copy Editor
Naomi W. Wolf
ASSISTANT: Patricia Cooper

148

ACKNOWLEDGMENTS

The Editors are indebted to Leonard V. Huber of New Orleans for his assistance in locating pictorial material and for the use of his private collection of photographs, and to his secretary, Mary A. Waits; also to Mrs. Ruth K. Field, Curator of the Pictorial History Gallery, Missouri Historical Society, St. Louis, who gave so generously of her time in researching material in that institution. In addition, they wish to thank the following individuals and organizations for their assistance and for making available pictorial material in their collections:

City Art Museum of St. Louis—Merritt S. Hitt, Thomas T. Hoopes

George Wilson, St. Louis

James Jerome Hill Reference Library, St. Paul—Russell F. Barnes

Louisiana State Museum, New Orleans—C. E. Frampton, D. Clive Hardy

Mercantile Library of St. Louis—Mary Dorward, Mrs. J. M. Hayes

Frederick Way, Jr., Sewickley, Pa.

Missouri Historical Society, St. Louis— Ruth Ferris

Waterways Journal, St. Louis—Capt. Donald T. Wright, Capt. Roy L. Barkhau

Photography of paintings and prints: New York—John D. Schiff; New Orleans—Charles F. Weber; St. Louis—Paul Piaget.

FOR FURTHER READING

Baldwin, Leland. *The Keelboat Age on the Mississippi.* University of Pittsburgh Press, 1941.

Banta, R. E. *The Ohio.* ("Rivers of America Series.") Rinehart, 1949.

Bissell, Richard. *High Water.* Little, Brown, 1954.

Bissell, Richard. *Monongahela.* ("Rivers of America Series.") Rinehart, 1952.

Blair, Walter, and Meine, Franklin. *Mike Fink, King of the Mississippi Keelboatmen.* Holt, 1933.

Botkin, Benjamin A. *Treasury of Mississippi Folklore.* Crown, 1951.

Burman, Ben. *Big River to Cross.* John Day, 1940.

Butler, Pierce. *The Unhurried Years.* Louisiana State University Press, 1948.

Carter, Hodding. *Lower Mississippi.* ("Rivers of America Series.") Rinehart, 1942.

Clemens, Samuel L. *Huckleberry Finn.* Globe, 1951.

Clemens, Samuel L. *Life on the Mississippi.* Harper, 1961.

Clemens, Samuel L. *Tom Sawyer.* E. P. Dutton, 1955.

Dorsey, Florence. *Master of the Mississippi, Henry Shreve and the Conquest of the Mississippi.* Houghton Mifflin, 1941.

Eifert, Virginia. *Delta Queen: The Story of a Steamboat.* Dodd, Mead, 1960.

Eskew, Garnett. *The Pageant of Packets.* Henry Holt, 1929.

Graham, Philip. *Showboats: The History of an American Institution.* University of Texas, 1951.

Hanson, Joseph M. *Conquest of the Missouri.* Rinehart, 1946.

Havighurst, Walter. *Upper Mississippi.* ("Rivers of America Series.") Rinehart, 1944.

Hunter, Louis. *Steamboats on the Western Rivers.* Harvard University Press, 1949.

Kane, Harnett. *Natchez on the Mississippi.* William Morrow, 1947.

Morrison, John. *History of American Steam Navigation.* Stephen Daye Press, 1958.

Quick, Herbert and Edward. *Mississippi Steamboatin'.* Henry Holt, 1926.

Rosskam, Edwin. *Towboat River.* Duell, Sloan & Pearce, 1948.

Russell, Charles. *A-Rafting on the Mississippi.* Century, 1928.

Samuel, Ray, Huber, Leonard, and Ogden, Warren. *Tales of the Mississippi.* Hastings House, 1955.

Vestal, Stanley. *The Missouri.* ("Rivers of America Series.") Rinehart, 1945.

Way, Frederick. *Allegheny.* ("Rivers of America Series.") Rinehart, 1942.

Way, Frederick. *The Log of the Betsy Ann.* McBride, 1933.

Way, Frederick. *Pilotin' Comes Natural.* Farrar & Rinehart, 1943.

Wellman, Manly. *Fastest on the River.* Henry Holt, 1957.

Index

Bold face indicates pages on which maps or illustrations appear

PEERLES

Manufacturers of the following Choice
BRANDS OF
Fine Cut
Chewing Tobacco.
VIZ.
PEERLESS.
BEAUTY.
VINEYARD.
STAR.
&c.

James Queen, del.

M. S. MEPH

977
A
AMERICAN HERITAGE
  Steamboats on the
  Mississippi

DATE DUE			
			ALESCO